MORE WAYS TO DISPLAY

A SECOND PRACTICAL GUIDE FOR TEACHERS

Derek Greenstreet

Illustrations: Derek Greenstreet

Ⓦ **Ward Lock Educational**

First published 1989 by
Ward Lock Educational Co. Ltd
T.R. House
1 Christopher Road
East Grinstead
Sussex RH19 3BT

A member of the Ling Kee group
HONG KONG · TAIPEI · SINGAPORE · LONDON · NEW YORK

British Library Cataloguing in Publication Data

Greenstreet, Derek
    More ways to display.
    1. Displays in education
    2. Education, Elementary — Audio-visual 8
    I. Title
    372.   13'3042   B1043.6

ISBN 07062 5107 5

Typeset by BLA Publishing Ltd.
Printed in Hong Kong

This book is dedicated to all teachers who consistently
strive to create stimulating and visually exciting
learning environments in their classrooms and to the
many children whose imaginative and spontaneous efforts
contribute to them.

Acknowledgements

*The author would like to thank the following people
for their assistance in the preparation of this book:*

The headteacher, staff and pupils of Beauherne CP
School, Canterbury, Kent; Grove Park CP School,
Sittingbourne, Kent, and in particular Mrs C Robertson;
Mr J Marshall and the students of Christ Church College
of Higher Education, Canterbury, Kent; and the many
teachers who have invited me into their schools and
requested help with aspects of display work; and finally
my wife Valerie, daughter Nicola, and son Matthew for
their patience, understanding, and encouragement during
the time spent compiling the text.

Contents

Introduction

This book is a sequel to *Ways to Display*, published by Ward Lock Educational in 1985. In that book I attempted to show why display is important as a means of enriching the learning environment for children in our schools, and the extent to which it can successfully be achieved without a disproportionate investment of time, effort and cost. Why then a second book? I have received a large number of requests both from experienced teachers and those in training for further guidance in establishing a school policy for the display and presentation of work.

Whilst all schools are different and often work hard to create their own particular ethos and approach, there are certain features that are fundamental and therefore common to all. Display is one such feature, because it represents an integral part of a teacher's work and responsibility and permeates the whole school. Seen in these terms, display becomes much more than simply arranging pieces of work on walls or hanging it from ceilings — although I would not in any way wish to underestimate the value of this important aspect of display. It is, however, only a small part of what display and presentation in schools is all about. In essence display becomes a vital part of the total learning environment of the school. The visual environment contributes to the level of care and respect for children's work that exists within a school. Concern for quality and excellence should be reflected in the kind of learning environment created.

For those readers not familiar with the original publication *Ways to Display*, here is a summary of the purpose of good display. I hope this will also serve as a link between the ideas covered in *Ways to Display* and those raised for the first time in this book.

The purpose of display

Good display should:

1. Make the learning environment visually stimulating and attractive.

2. Communicate ideas and information clearly and appropriately.

3. Encourage interest and stimulate questions and discussion.

4. Show the extent to which children's work is valued and appreciated by the whole school community.

5. Respond to the interests of the children.

6. Reflect the general ethos of the class and the wider context of the school.

7. Provide opportunities for the sharing of ideas between pupils, staff and visitors.

8. Enrich the learning experience of all the children.

9. Help towards an understanding of different cultural backgrounds.

10. Provide both an additional and alternative learning resource in the classroom.

Teachers are very busy people. The demands made upon them increase constantly, making it more and more important to find effective ways of helping them to achieve attractive and purposeful displays as part of their normal classroom work. Much time and effort can be saved if teachers have the right materials and equipment to hand, and some knowledge and understanding of basic display techniques.

Make the learning environment attractive.

Materials and equipment

Access to the following materials and equipment help to make display attractive and quick to produce.

MATERIALS

Papers
Assorted colours of sugar paper, frieze paper, poster or mounting paper, newsprint, cartridge paper, printers' offcuts. (Please note that neutral colours and not bright colours generally produce better backgrounds, e.g. black, white, grey, beige, buff.)

Card
White and assorted colours of 3, 6 and 12-sheet thickness, manilla, corrugated, and extra thick mounting card. (The latter is usually coloured on one side and white on the reverse. It is very expensive and therefore generally reserved for specially selected pieces of work.)

Packaging
A good source of large pieces of sandwich construction board suitable for making display boards.

Adhesives
PVA, wallpaper paste (Polycell), Pritt stick, Cowgum, fabric adhesive (Copydex).

Fixings
Mapping pins, dress-making pins, Blu-Tack, double-sided vinyl tape, coloured vinyl tape, double-sided adhesive pads, masking tape, staples, matt finish vinyl tape, fishing line, eyelets.

Markers and colours
Water and spirit-based markers, drawing inks, Brusho colour, posterpaint, powder paint, pastels, crayons, italic markers.

Miscellaneous
Paper-backed hessian, display felt, netting, fabric drapes, bricks, wood shelving, ceramic pots/vases.

Equipment

Tools
Rotary trimmer, cutting knives, safety rulers, scissors, paper shears, staplers (Bambi, table, long arm), staple gun, hook stapler (Turikan), ram pin, cutting board, pliers, staple remover, T-square, combined hole punch and eyelet tool, hot wire cutter, glue gun.

Suitability of materials
Regular handling is the most satisfactory way of discovering what various materials are suitable for, but for the inexperienced it is helpful to understand some basic principles in order to avoid wasting time and money. I hope the following suggestions will save some frustration and disappointment.

1. Backing paper should always be of heavier quality than the piece of work being attached to it. This will eliminate the risk of wrinkles, creases, and air bubbles forming.

2. Avoid using reflective materials in displays (e.g. drawing pins, clear vinyl sticking tape).

3. Use spirit-based markers or waterproof colours (e.g. drawing inks) where work is likely to get splashed and cause the colours to run.

4. Match adhesives to other materials carefully (e.g. for sticking paper to paper use wallpaper paste; for sticking paper to cardboard use diluted PVA; for sticking cardboard to cardboard use 'neat' PVA).

5. Whenever possible cover display boards with hessian to disguise pinholes and avoid the need to constantly change backing paper.

6. Most coloured papers fade if left in direct sunlight; displays need positioning carefully.

A selection of display equipment

General principles of successful display

To conclude, I suggest the following general principles for successfully displaying children's work. Whether or not they can be met in full will depend upon individual situations, but they do provide a sound basis by which teachers can assess the merit of their display work.

1. Let children see you handle their work with respect and care. This means mounting and arranging it thoughtfully.

2. Change all displays as regularly as possible; they cease to make an impact if they remain in position for too long' and become 'tatty' in appearance.

3. Whenever possible arrange display work at an easy viewing height for children and in good light.

4. Make sure that all work is accurately trimmed, well mounted and carefully aligned.

5. Displays should not be overcrowded; work requires space and careful arrangement if it is to attract attention and have visual appeal.

6. Headings, titles, captions and labels all require clear and well-formed lettering.

7. Plain backgrounds of neutral colours are usually most successful for displays; bright and patterned backgrounds are often confusing and distracting.

8. Geometric arrangements are visually easier to assimilate; aim for a balance between large and small pieces of work.

9. Whenever possible involve the child in the selection of work to be displayed.

10. It is essential to make the intention of the display easily recognisable.

11. Displays should not only be regarded as the conclusion to work achieved; they often act as starting points to initiate new or further work.

'Creating visual displays of work and items of interest allows teachers and children the opportunity to apply a measure of control to their working environment: they can put their unique "stamp" upon their immediate surroundings.'

ILEA Teachers' Art Centre

Well-formed lettering is important.

The interior of a display should be clear.

A Whole School Policy for Display

Most teachers are now familiar with examining various aspects of school effectiveness from the point of view of formulating a 'whole school policy.' As a continuing process, many schools review areas of their curriculum in order to establish better progression through the school and to generally enrich the quality of teaching and learning. Staff development programmes have been introduced to encourage teachers to work more closely together as a team, while at the same time fostering their own individuality and strengths. In addition to matters of organisation, curriculum, and staff development, schools are being positively encouraged to think about the importance of school image and ethos. A major part of this particular debate concerns the quality and purpose of display and presentation in the school.

I have been asked on a number of occasions over the past two or three years to talk to and lead discussions with various groups of teachers and headteachers on matters relating to 'Creating learning environments for children.' This includes principles of display and presentation. For school staff to give attention to this area of concern as a matter of policy indicates the level of importance attached to it and consequently it assumes a role comparable with staff and curriculum development. This immediately raises fundamental questions: Why display? For whom is it intended? What purpose does it achieve? To what extent does it affect children's learning? Is the class and school environment important? Does it contribute to the ethos of the whole school? Does it help to enrich the quality of both teaching and learning? Is the time and effort justified?

These are typical questions being asked by teachers about the display and presentation of children's work.

Later in this chapter I include a summary of one school's approach to establishing a policy for display and presentation. However, as a starting point I intend to make a closer examination of the principles involved and suggest ways of drawing good examples of individual practice into the formulation of a 'whole school policy.'

In the introduction to this book I have already attempted to establish why high standards of display and presentation should be an essential part of a teacher's classroom responsibility. In this chapter I shall consider some of the other, as yet, unanswered questions. Clearly there is a need for teachers to fully understand the purpose of display and to be quite sure that their aims are met. Planning a display is therefore an essential element of the much bigger task of planning a topic or sequence of work. Whilst such planning is frequently undertaken by individual teachers and related solely to the class of children for whom they are responsible, other schools plan on a 'whole school basis.' This often involves a common topic or theme being explored throughout the school at the same time, and the planning may therefore include consideration of the kind of stimulus display required to initiate the work and the way different aspects of the topic or theme will be represented in the various displays around the school.

A policy of this kind implies the need to think ahead, build up supplies of adequate resources, and to draw sketch plans of how individual displays are visualised so that a cohesive pattern can be established across the whole school. This may, of course, involve teachers taking responsibility for central or shared areas of the school in addition to their own classrooms. In this way, the work of one class may influence the work of another, so that the whole school becomes caught up in an exchange of interpretations and ideas. In schools where this happens most effectively, work by children of different ages and from different classes is displayed side by side. Whilst the content of such a display has much in common, the interpretation differs greatly and this provides a valuable opportunity for staff and pupils to cultivate a 'whole school view' of what is being achieved.

Sharing of experience

Fundamental to the entire question of 'whole school policy' is the fact that teachers should contribute to open sharing of experience. This is accepted in all areas of curriculum development, but it would be equally beneficial for display and presentation. Teachers should be encouraged to visit each others' classrooms (and schools whenever possible) to observe alternative approaches to display, pool ideas, and share solutions for overcoming problems. In schools where this happens consistently, the result is an overall rise in the standard of display and presentation throughout the school. Whilst this directly affects the whole ethos of the school, perhaps the most far-reaching effect is on the children's learning. A learning environment that is dynamic, stimulating and exciting, where great trouble has been taken to arrange visual material with care and a sense of order, influences the way children respond to learning and the quality of presentation of their own written and illustrated work.

Storage of materials

Many teachers prefer to build up their own resources for displays. Over a period of time it is possible to collect all kinds of interesting and useful items, although storage frequently presents a problem. Some schools choose, as part of their policy, to centralise the material available for display purposes and devise ways of storing it by adapting and utilising otherwise wasted spaces in odd corners, under stairwells, or converted cloakrooms around the school. In the last school in which I was headteacher a room designated as a book store was adapted and used for this purpose. It often takes only a little vision, determination, time and effort to change the function of available facilities. Many schools, even those that on the surface appear very cramped, have spaces that can be used differently.

By adopting the centralised approach materials become available and can be added to by all the staff. Considerable time can be wasted searching for such items, particularly if staff have little idea where they are likely to locate them. The central collection may contain such things as:

1. Lengths of fabric for use as drapes.

2. Rolls of corrugated card or fabric for skirting tables.

3. Assorted containers and display stands for isolating particular exhibits in a display.

4. Large vases or sections of pipe for displaying dried grasses or flowers.

5. Collections of animal bones and skulls, feathers, shells, fossils, pebbles, mounted butterflies and moths — and a host of other items that may be considered useful to enrich the classroom environment.

A school gallery

Children gain much benefit from seeing each others' work. The benefit is increased if they are encouraged by their teacher to discuss the merits of the work. A successful way of achieving this is to have a school gallery situated in a convenient place such as the assembly hall or a long expanse of corridor wall. The gallery display should ideally consist of a picture (more than one if space allows) from each class in the school, representing the youngest to the oldest children. The pictures can be displayed in card window mounts, which allow work to be easily changed so that different pictures can be shown each week or fortnight. The children can actively be involved in the selection of pictures to be displayed. On occasions, to add variety, it may be possible to have the same theme or subject running throughout the school so that the gallery display shows different responses, by different ages of children, to the same theme. In the chapter dealing with exhibitions there are suggestions for extending this idea for a wider audience.

School policy in relation to display may be extremely detailed, whilst in some schools it may be non-existent. I know of schools which detail such matters as the frequency with which displays are changed; the kind of fixings to be used when displaying work on boards

and walls; the colour of mounts to be used in displays; whether or not work should be single, double or triple mounted; and the kind of backing material to be used.

Schools known to me have raised money to enable all display boards throughout the school to be covered with paper-backed hessian. Whilst this is initially more expensive, overall it is cheaper as new backing paper does not have to be used every time a display is put up.

Central or shared areas

School policy varies greatly when it comes to displays that are situated in areas other than classrooms. Entrance halls, assembly halls, foyers, corridors, stairways and landings are very much public areas and therefore shared by the whole school community. Such areas can easily become a 'no man's land', with no one in particular taking responsibility for coordinating the display in them. They soon become neglected areas, either devoid of display altogether or accommodating outdated, unchanged work that has faded with age and ceased to interest the children. A clearly defined plan is needed to prevent this happening. There are various ways of overcoming the problem. In some schools, individual classes (teachers and children) take responsibility for particular display boards or areas of the school. Alternatively, classes housed in a particular wing or part of the school arrange all the displays within the vicinity of their classrooms. Often a common theme is shared between the contributing classes, with one teacher taking the responsibility for coordinating the displays. Other schools organise the distribution on a yeargroup or school team basis, with work from the various sources being sent to a designated member of staff who coordinates the final setting up of the displays.

Many schools get parents to help with mounting the work (under the guidance of the teacher), leaving members of staff to arrange the display and add any additional features.

Tools for the job

Part of the centralised collection of materials referred to earlier could consist of suitable tools for setting up displays. In small schools this seldom creates many difficulties, but in larger schools teachers frequently become frustrated when they are unable to locate the tools they require! The most satisfactory system is to equip each teacher with a basic display kit. Whilst this is initially very much more expensive and will probably need to be built up over a period of time, it enables teachers to create their displays much more quickly and is consequently self-motivating. If finances will not permit this, then a kit would need to be shared between a small group of teachers. The kit might consist of the following items: Trigger Tacker staple gun, Bambi size stapler, ram pin tool, staple remover, large pair of craft scissors, dress-making pins, mapping pins, nylon thread, cutting knife, and safety ruler. The kit could be kept in a simple plastic tool/storage box obtainable from most DIY chainstores. There is a more comprehensive list of useful tools and materials at the end of this book.

Lettering

In many schools, a valuable feature of a display is the degree of individuality that the various members of staff provide. An imaginative and personal style is to be encouraged as an excepted part of a school policy for display, but there are some attributes that should be regarded as beneficial if adopted by the whole or particular parts of the school. Styles of lettering used in headings or titles is one such example. It cannot be assumed that all children can cope with elaborate or decorative letter forms that may look visually attractive but fail to have meaning for them. It is often more appropriate to relate the lettering in displays to those styles with which they are familiar. In infant departments simple print script as found in most early readers or hand writing schemes is a suitable style to adopt for displays. The absence of capital letters may also be an accepted feature. Older children, more used to observing alternative styles of lettering in advertisements and the media generally, are likely to be able to cope with a variety of letter forms and not find them confusing or distracting. A degree of school policy in this respect can be helpful.

A school policy statement for display

The following statement, describing one Kent school's policy for display, has been written by the school's consultant for art, design, and display. It provides a clear and helpful insight into the way in which 'creating the right kind of learning environment' is regarded as an integral part of the school's approach to teaching and learning.

'This brief summary describes the policy for display in a large county primary school set on the edge of a private housing estate, surrounded by fields, woodland and parkland and having its own small nature reserve and pond and being within walking distance of the local church and town.

It is within this setting, with all the resources that it has to offer, that as a staff we are committed to the belief that firsthand experience is fundamental to the development of work of quality across the curriculum. This is clearly reflected in the value which is attached to carefully arranged and thoughtfully sited displays throughout the school which provide a background for an educational philosophy which has the aesthetic and creative development and enrichment of children as its central core.

Within individual classrooms, displays of work reflect the specific interests of the children and are used to stimulate questioning, promote interest and extend work in a number of directions so as to make the classroom a more exciting and attractive place in which to work. Along with the children's work, the display will often contain source material from which the work has developed. This may include a combination of natural and manmade materials, such as real objects, photographs and models.

As the school is semi open plan, displays are linked from classroom to corridor, library to entrance hall and into the main assembly hall. There is an intentional flow of display, linking infant and junior work, so as to show the developmental progression which is of interest to both staff and the pupils themselves.

Much of the display is arranged on a thematic basis. With an emphasis on progression and continuity in all areas of the curriculum there is always a relationship established within the display.

The real effectiveness of display throughout the school has essentially depended upon the measure of care and planning invested in it on the part of all the staff. We all feel that to give due respect to the children's efforts by displaying their work with sensitivity demands time, thought, effort and teamwork.

The learning and sharing together as a team of teachers has been an integral part of building our school policy for display. In structuring a display considerations of colour, design, texture and scale are discussed together. All colours and textures are blended together and an interest in different levels, angles and lighting is carefully considered. The use of fabric drapes for backdrops, lengths of coloured hessian, pots for displaying grasses and flowers and collections of all kinds of interesting objects are encouraged as being useful additions to good display. Adjacent to most displays in the school relevant reading material is often placed for the children to borrow and extend their interest.

Sometimes, as part of a display, items of adult work are added to show the use of materials, different styles of working or viewpoints. This contributes to the beginnings of critical analysis and aesthetic appreciation.

When considering as a staff how a display should be put together, methods of mounting and suitability of materials are discussed. This is frequently arranged as a 'workshop' and in working together we learn from each other.

It is this personal interest of caring teachers presenting children's work with a visual sensitivity that provides us all, teachers, children and parents, with an ever-changing, exciting and stimulating environment in which to work and visit. Display is not regarded as an impressionable piece of window dressing but as a vital part of the children's learning experience.'

Good display should arouse curiosity and questioning by enriching the learning experience.

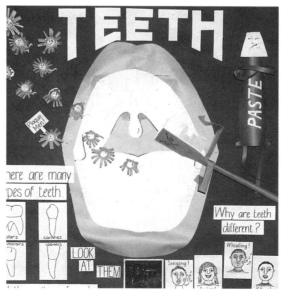

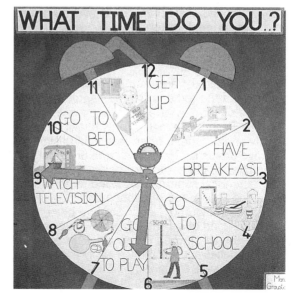

Arranging and Organising the Classroom for Display

Lack of space for displaying work is one of the major difficulties that teachers have to contend with in creating a stimulating learning environment. Few schools are well equipped with fixed display boards, suitable spot lighting, and movable display units for showing three-dimensional work to advantage. Often rooms are overcrowded, cluttered with excess or inappropriate furniture, and have vertical surfaces broken up by pipes, cables, and sockets or made from materials that make the fixing of display work a nightmare! This chapter will consider ways of achieving successful display in difficult situations and with as little cost as possible. Engaging the help of the PTA in providing funds and labour can often help to transform the aesthetic appearance of specific areas of a school. Help of this kind is often of longer-lasting benefit than individual acquisitions that only offer short-term improvement.

Storage

Storage is almost always a problem in schools. Teachers tend to hoard large quantities of materials that may at a later date prove 'to be useful'! Though the logic of this thinking can be easily understood, it often results in unsightly storage problems. Nothing is more unattractive than piles of old cardboard boxes, obtained from the local supermarket, piled under work surfaces and on top of cupboards.

Brightly-coloured, plastic storage boxes can be purchased quite cheaply from DIY stores. These can be stacked on or under horizontal work surfaces and still remain easily accessible. Simple racking, made from either stained or painted battening, can be built in under work

surfaces so that the boxes can be stored separately, rather than on top of each other, to make access even easier. The boxes can be clearly labelled using either pen lettering or 'jumbo' tape embossed lettering made with an embossed lettering machine.

If it is not possible to purchase a storage system of this kind and cardboard boxes have to be used, it is a good idea to spend some time making them more durable and attractive. A team of parents could form a working party to undertake a project of this kind. If an arrangement can be made with a local store or supermarket to keep boxes of a particular type so that size and strength is standardised it is possible to create a very neat and economical storage system. The boxes can be covered

Stout cardboard box, covered with paper-backed hessian and reinforced with plastic spine binders around the top edges

with paper-backed hessian, which is both visually attractive and tough, or any other suitable covering material such as adhesive-backed plastic or decorative papers, depending on the amount of money available. PVA adhesive will fix most covering materials securely. To prevent the top edges of the boxes from becoming damaged it is worth glueing plastic spine binders along them, having first mitred the corners to give a neat finish.

Odd rolls of paper-backed hessian are sometimes available at reduced prices from home decorating and DIY stores.

For large, bulky objects more robust storage boxes can be made that double as three-dimensional display units. Boxes made from plywood, on a light batten framework with either a removable top or hinged-side locker-type doors are very functional and look most attractive if stained and varnished or painted. The top surface can be covered with tiles of cork, carpet, vinyl, or thin parquet flooring. Storage boxes of this kind are very expensive to buy from educational suppliers but can easily be made by DIY parent enthusiasts for a fraction of the cost. Old desks can be adapted in a similar way by boxing them in with plywood or Sundela pinboard covered with hessian, creating both additional storage space and a display surface at the same time. If required, the board fixed to the back of the desk can be extended so as to make a high-level display board above the horizontal surface of the desktop so that two-and three-dimensional work can be displayed together. Two boxed-in desks can be arranged back to back with a display board between them so that they form an island display that can be viewed from all sides. Locker doors can be incorporated to provide storage underneath the desks.

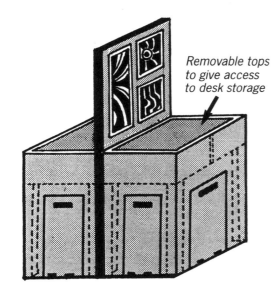

Removable tops to give access to desk storage

Boxed in desks with locker-type doors to give storage underneath

Shelves

Shelves are not usually the most attractive feature of any classroom as they tend to harbour materials that are not in regular demand. With a little imagination and effort, however, they can be adapted to provide additional display and storage facilities. A strip of beading tacked along the front edge of a shelf allows artwork, mounted in card window

frames, to be arranged along the full length of the shelf. Similarly work can be hung in front of the shelves, masking simple storage boxes housed underneath the shelves and made to slide on wooden runners. Like the storage boxes previously described, these can easily be made by parents or other willing helpers who have basic carpentry skills.

A shelf mounted along the bottom of a vertical wall display board is extremely useful in providing a link between two-and three-dimensional aspects of a display. Cutout card strip, appropriately painted, can be fixed along the front and ends of a shelf. Three-dimensional work can then be arranged on the shelf against a background of two-dimensional work on the same theme displayed on the wall board.

Suitable themes might include seascapes, landscapes, jungle habitats, houses and

gardens, townscapes, space scenes, or any other subject matter that would benefit from a display that relies on depth for its success.

Similarly, mounting a shelf along both the top and bottom of a wall display board extends the possibilities even further in terms of creating depth displays. Work displayed on the wall board forms the background, whilst work arranged on the bottom shelf or hung from the top shelf in the form of mobiles serves as middle distance images. The foreground can then be made up from work attached to the front edges of the two shelves, creating an overall impression of distance and depth. Depending on the theme of the display, the two sides can be filled in by attaching more cutout images to the ends of the two shelves. This further emphasises the three-dimensional aspect of the display, almost giving it a sense of theatre.

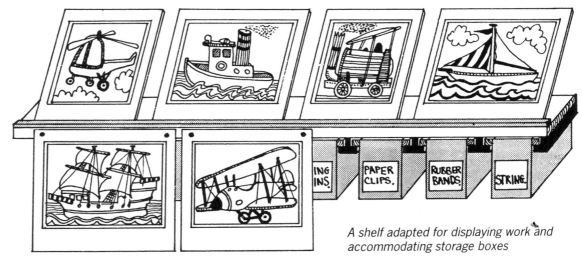

A shelf adapted for displaying work and accommodating storage boxes

Display mounted on a vertical wall board with a shelf positioned above and below

If the classroom is to be an attractive and ordered environment it is important that children should know where things are and where they should be returned. A good system of storage that is clearly understood by everyone is therefore essential. Swing-bin type containers, with the tops removed if necessary, make excellent storage places for such things as pieces of fabric (arranged according to colour), or junk materials sorted into categories (e.g. small boxes, plastic containers, cardboard tubes, wood offcuts). Each bin should be clearly labelled and possibly colour coded for easy identification by very young children.

Display space

Two-dimensional work

If no fixed display boards are available there are a number of alternatives for displaying two-dimensional work. Fixing lengths of 'L'

section moulding in wood, plastic, or aluminium to walls provides a satisfactory means of hanging two-dimensional work that has been mounted in card window mounts. The work can be stood on the horizontal face of the moulding and lent against the wall. Or it may be hung from the moulding using small 'S' shaped hooks made from bent wire. These may be put in holes drilled in the horizontal

Two-dimensional work standing on 'L' section moulding

Two-dimensional work hung from 'S' shaped hooks

face of the moulding or in punched holes in the top corners of the window mounts.

This type of arrangement provides good display opportunities in the classroom and is also very suitable for corridors and assembly halls where a long run of display can give an impressive gallery effect.

Central displays

If space permits, then it may be possible to have a central display as a feature of the classroom. This kind of display becomes a focal point for the children seated around it and a point of reference for the teacher, who can refer to it more easily as a teaching aid.

A column-type structure, made from cardboard boxes decreasing in size, can be assembled in a tower formation. The boxes can be covered with paper-backed hessian, or a similar material. The vertical surfaces on all

Column structure with flat boards inserted between the boxes and rotatated through 45°

Column structure made from strong cardboard boxes covered with decorative paper or hessian

four sides provide display space for two-dimensional work, whilst the horizontal surfaces can be attractively arranged with three-dimensional work.

Variety can be added to the tower structure by introducing a flat sheet of stout card or thin board (plywood or hardboard) suitably covered with coloured paper, hessian, or display felt, between each level of the structure. This provides additional visual interest and more space for three-dimensional display.

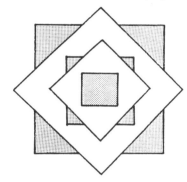

Aerial view of column structures using different shaped units

The strong cardboard tubes from the centre of rolls of carpet or vinyl floor covering make excellent round display units. The tubes can be sawn into appropriate lengths, using a fine toothed saw, to give display units of different levels. Flat discs of card can be stuck on one end of the tube to provide the surface on which to display three-dimensional objects. The whole shape then needs to be covered with paper-backed hessian, corrugated card, or decorative paper. Hexagonal and octagonal forms can be made by simply scoring and folding strips of stout card into the required

shape, remembering to make allowance for an additional section to act as a 'tab' for fixing the shape together. Shapes of this kind, made from different coloured card or covered with

1	2	3	4	5	6	7	8	Tab

Card scored and folded into eight sections, plus tab for making octagonal shape

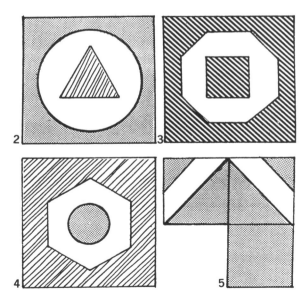

Column structures can be assembled using different combinations of shapes.

coordinating coloured papers can greatly enhance the appearance of a display.

The ceiling

The ceiling is normally a far from ideal place to mount a display, except for hanging mobiles. But this very large space can sometimes be used to advantage. It is not always easy to view work clearly at such a height, but the following are examples of appropriate ceiling displays.

A very successful and impressive display was created in the classroom by lower junior-aged children following a visit to Canterbury Cathedral. During the visit the children became fascinated by the vast arrangement of heraldic ceiling bosses (over eight hundred of them) around the cloisters. On returning to school the children were keen to recreate the effect in their own classroom. They made delightful heraldic shields and coats-of-arms in relief, using cardboard and adhesive, which were then decorated and displayed on the classroom and adjacent corridor ceiling. It would have been difficult to find a more appropriate place for this display.

In another classroom the whole ceiling was transformed into a giant compass. All the directional points of the compass were marked around the ceiling in a most decorative way to assist the children with a local study project. The children had found difficulty in establishing the correct direction when referring to landmarks and features in the vicinity of the school. The ceiling space was therefore effectively used to provide a permanent reminder.

In a similar way ceiling displays could be developed for a variety of topics such as space, the universe, planets, the solar system, or the history of aviation.

Adapting and improving

Teachers frequently find they have to adapt existing furniture and equipment to new uses. This is certainly true when it comes to finding appropriate ways of displaying work in the classroom and around the school. In schools so often ill-equipped with good display facilities, teachers have to find alternative ways of achieving display space and suitable surfaces. This was dealt with briefly in *Ways to Display*, and here I offer further suggestions.

Table and desktop displays

It is surprising how, with a little imagination and effort, a seemingly unattractive table or desk can be turned into a very acceptable display unit using not much more than pieces of fabric and card.

The table can be 'skirted' in a number of ways depending upon the materials available or the cost involved. Rolls of corrugated cardboard, preferably coloured, can be wrapped around the legs to completely surround it. This not only makes it visually more attractive, but also provides additional vertical surfaces on which two-dimensional work can be attached using dress-making pins. The table does not have to be fully skirted but can have a half skirt attached, cut into an interesting shape at the bottom edge.

The tabletop can be covered with either coloured paper or fabric.

Ends of rolls of fabric, or remnants, also make useful skirting material for display units and can be obtained quite cheaply, especially

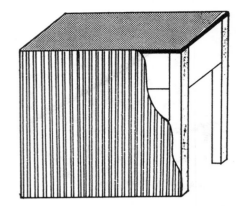

Skirting a table with corrugated cardboard

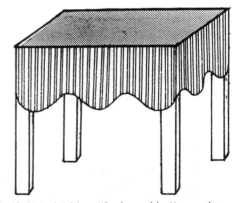

A half-skirted table with shaped bottom edge

from market stalls. The material can either be draped over the table as a tablecloth, or gathered around the whole table and fixed with a staple gun.

A quicker and more satisfactory way of achieving the same effect is to cut and hem the fabric to the right length and height and staple it to a width of card that has been scored and folded to fit the shape of the table.

It can then be simply pinned to the table from underneath the fabric and used time and time again.

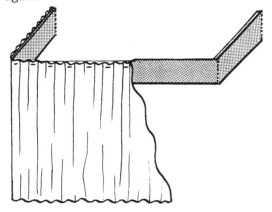

The skirt can be made to mask either three or four sides of the desk or table.

A very cheap yet satisfactory way of skirting the legs of desks and tables for display purposes is by using the cardboard from large packaging cases (e.g. the kind used for washing machines and dishwashers). These are made of corrugations sandwiched between two sheets of flat card. The tops and bottoms of the cases should be removed, leaving only the four sides. As it is unlikely that the packaging case will be of the precise dimensions required to fit around the desk or table it should be adapted in the following way:

1. Cut the packaging case to the correct height using a sharp knife and straight edge.

2. Cut down two of the corners of the packaging case, leaving two large sections of cardboard each with a centrefold.

3. These can then be trimmed to size to fit the dimensions of the desk or table.

4. Rejoin the two sections using wide single-sided self-adhesive carpet tape.

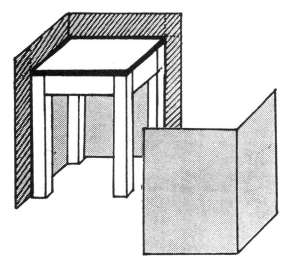

Desk showing cardboard packaging in position around two sides. The shaded area indicates the part to be cut away.

The resulting sleeve will now slide exactly over the desk or table, masking it as required. The surface can be decorated with paper-backed hessian, providing additional display space that will accept pins and staples. Paper-backed hessian is the most satisfactory covering material because, unlike smooth papers, it will not show pinholes.

The sleeve will fold almost flat for storage purposes — although most display units tend to be in constant use once they have been produced!

Creating bays

There are many alternatives to simply arranging display material on flat horizontal surfaces. If the display is to be sited in a central position, then viewing it from more than one angle becomes possible. A horizontal display surface can be divided in a number of ways by using scored and glued card to provide a variety of display possibilities. The following illustrations show ways of dividing horizontal display surfaces in order to create bays and different interest areas.

Here the horizontal display surface has been divided into two bays using either cut down packaging cases or sheets of scored and folded card that have been covered with coloured paper or hessian. Note how the sides of B have been cut away to form triangular shapes, whereas those in A have been left as rectangles.

Sloping and stepped display units

An alternative to dividing the horizontal surface into bays is to build up sloping or stepped display units, again either using strong cardboard (corrugated sandwich board from packing cases), hardboard, thin plywood, or Sundela pinboard. Assembly may take a number of forms, as illustrated, depending upon whether two- or three-dimensional work is to be displayed. If it is intended for three-dimensional work, the sloping surface can be stepped to provide horizontal platforms by using thick scored and folded card that can be attached to the existing surfaces with mapping pins or double-sided self-adhesive pads. It is also helpful to tack a small strip of beading or moulding around the edge of the horizontal surface to ensure that the raised display unit cannot move and risk being damaged.

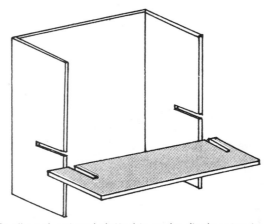

Cardboard, cut and slotted to make display stands

Sloping and stepped display units

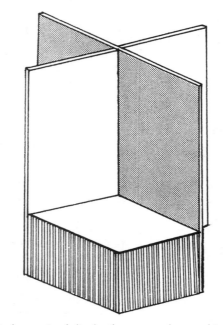

Note how raised display boxes can be used in conjunction with stands of this kind.

Slot and assemble

Other fascinating and effective desk or tabletop display units can be made by using the 'slot and assemble' method. Using a sharp craft knife cut slots across half the width of a piece of card. Cut further slots halfway across the width of another piece of card to be joined to the first in a corresponding position. Line up the slots and snap the two pieces of card together to give a strong and stable structure. With this method it is possible to assemble all kinds of interesting shapes that make exciting display units for three-dimensional work. A variety of combinations can be achieved using different coloured card. When not required for display, the pieces can be unslotted and stored flat.

Adapting unwanted household items

A newsletter to parents appealing for unwanted items of household equipment, offcuts of wood and other useful materials — plus a small team of helpers willing to undertake simple carpentry and wield a paint brush — should provide other display ideas.

A vertical clothes'-horse, of the telescopic folding kind, can easily be converted into an attractive and effective display unit for three-dimensional work. Pieces of cut wood can be assembled across the dowel rods to make a versatile shelved display unit. The shelves can each be painted a different colour, or in coordinating colours to contrast with the frame. If preferred, natural wood shelves could be fitted, giving the frame one or two coats of polyurethane clear varnish or wood stain.

An old horizontal wooden clothes'-horse, with either two or three sections, can also be

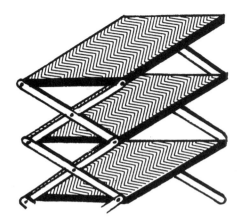

The weight of the wooden shelves makes this display unit stable and robust.

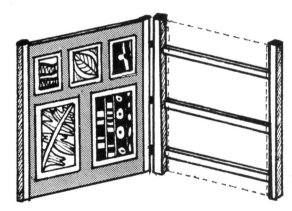

The vertical posts of a horizontal clothes-horse can be stained or varnished.

converted into a display stand for two-dimensional work. Screw Sundela pinboard onto each side of the wooden frames to make a substantial, free standing display board. A two-section clothes'-horse can be arranged at an angle of 90° to mask a corner or make a background around a display box. A three-section clothes'-horse, covered in the same way, can be folded to make a bay, an L-shaped unit or a triangular unit.

Blackboards

Blackboards, particularly of the two-or three-section sliding variety, often dominate a classroom. They take up a disproportionate amount of space and yet are seldom fully used. It is comparatively easy to make up Sundela pinboards on wooden battens that can be hung over sections of the blackboard that are not being used. The two outside sections of a blackboard might be used for display in this way with just the middle section remaining for normal use between them.

The same technique can be applied to roller boards, which are equally large and take up space that could be used more productively.

Furniture

Furniture can often be used to double as display space. I dealt with this topic in *Ways to Display*, and it is not my intention to repeat the same material other than to remind readers that it is often possible to achieve a more imaginative arrangement of the furniture and still leave as much, if not more, floor space to move about in. By moving furniture away from the walls and placing it at right angles the doors, sides, and back of the classroom become potential display spaces. Covered with materials such as cork tiles, carpet tiles, pinboard, corrugated cardboard or even polystyrene tiles painted with emulsion, unattractive and often dilapidated furniture can double as useful display space.

Disguising ugly walls

Often classroom walls are cluttered with a motley collection of ugly pipes and cables. They can easily spoil the visual appearance of the room unless some attempt is made to disguise them. This can be achieved by fixing short lengths of curtain rail on the wall and hanging fabric drapes over the offending eyesores. Remnants and ends of rolls can often be purchased at a reasonable price from soft-furnishing stores, market stalls, or even local authority departments that have their own supplies organisation and will sell oddments to schools. Alternatively, rolls of coloured corrugated cardboard can be opened out and used as a masking material to hide pipes and cables, and at the same time provide a surface to which two-dimensional work can be pinned for display.

Careful arrangement is essential.

Making the Most of Materials

Throughout this book I refer to the wide variety of materials that are useful for displaying work in schools. This chapter explores more fully how those materials can be used to make the display of children's work more attractive and effective. It is surprising how quite unexpected materials can be used to enrich the visual environment of a classroom.

This aspect of a teacher's work requires imagination to see how materials can be used to their best advantage. Some materials will have to be bought, but others can be obtained free or for very little cost.

A newsletter to parents can produce a variety of materials suitable for display purposes. Parents often do not realise that they have anything useful to offer, but in my own experience the following materials have been provided: carpet squares, carpet tiles, cork tiles, polystyrene tiles, card, paper, remnants of fabric, house plants, shelving and display felt — to name but a few. Also ask non-teaching staff such as the caretaker, groundsman, and canteen staff to save scrap materials that would otherwise be thrown away. All these materials can be used to improve the visual environment of the school and enhance the quality of display.

The following table suggests a range of materials suitable for display purposes and their possible uses, grouped under five headings: natural; man-made; building; scrap; miscellaneous.

These ideas are in no way conclusive; they simply represent some of the ways in which a wide range of materials can be used. Many of the materials are readily available and teachers will, of course, have many additional ideas of their own. I would suggest that these should be recorded in a methodical way so that they become common knowledge to all teachers in the school rather then remaining confined to individual teachers. Resource lists, perhaps tabulated in a similar way to the examples given here, could be a very helpful addition to any school policy and information document. In loose leaf form, they can be added to as new ideas are considered and tried. Teachers should also be encouraged to visit each others' rooms.

NATURAL MATERIALS	POSSIBLE USE IN DISPLAY
Dried grasses, dried flowers, house plants	Use in stimulus displays, arrangements in entrance halls, stairwells, landings, hanging baskets, etc.
Collections of seeds and fruits such as acorns, fir cones, conkers, dried beans, gourds	Use in touch or colour displays. Display on tin lids that have been edged with coloured vinyl tape and have a mat of coloured paper in the base. Alternatively display in clear glass containers with coloured lids, each clearly labelled.
Logs, slices of tree-trunks, bark, driftwood	Use as display stands or as objects to be touched in surfaces and textures touch displays. Slices of tree-trunk make attractive display stands for claywork, particularly based on natural objects.
Slate, pebbles, pieces of stone	Use in stimulus displays or as display stands.
Animal skulls, bones, fossils	Use in stimulus displays.
Stuffed birds and animals, feathers	Use as centrepieces for displays of animals, birds, habitats, wild life, flight, etc.
Shells, coral, sand	Use in stimulus displays. Sand provides a good base for a horizontal three-dimensional display.

MAN-MADE MATERIALS	POSSIBLE USE IN DISPLAY
Tins, boxes, polystyrene packaging, cardboard packaging, nets, baskets, trugs, bottles, jars of various shapes, sizes and colours, rope, tyres, wheels	Use for holding small items in stimulus displays, display stands, making simple pinboards and centrepieces for stimulus displays.
Carpet tiles, polystyrene tiles, cork tiles, hessian, textured wallpaper	Use to create pinboards on the sides, back, and doors of cupboards.
Fabric remnants, wall hangings, curtains	Use as table coverings, drapes or backdrops for displays.
Old picture frames	Can be sprayed, painted or stained. Use to feature the 'Picture of the Week' (or month), or simply hang empty in front of part of a display to focus attention on images seen through it.
Artificial grass, sheets and pieces of foam or sponge	Use as a base in environmental displays, or cut up to provide contours or multi-level effects. (Foam and sponge can be coloured using Brusho colour.)
Black polythene refuse sacks	Opened out or cut into thin strips they are excellent for creating caves and shelters in the corners of classrooms (e.g. witches and Hallowe'en themes).
Expanding garden trellis, thick bamboo canes, small fencing panels, loading pallets	Use to provide vertical display space as background arrangements.
Collections of various artefacts such as machines or machine parts, Victoriana, masks, carvings, museum pieces, etc.	Use as starting points in stimulus displays.
Old tools, farm implements, household items, historical memorabilia.	Use as starting points in historical displays.

A triangular tabletop display unit made from sandwich construction corrugated packaging. The joining sides can be taped on the inside and flat sheet card cut to shape and size placed on the top for three-dimensional display. Covered with paper-backed hessian the pinholes are disguised in the open weave. A neat finish can be obtained by edging the unit with card strip.

Clear glass jars make neat storage containers for small objects in displays.

House bricks, used in conjunction with polished or stained wood to make a shelved display unit.

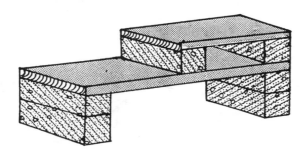

Display stands made from ceramic or plastic pipes with cut discs of coloured card stuck on top. (The card should be of a slightly larger diameter than the pipe.)

BUILDING MATERIALS	POSSIBLE USES IN DISPLAY
Bricks (a variety of colours and textures), concrete blocks, roof tiles, ceramic and plastic pipes, timber (planed, unplaned, stained, polished, etc.)	Use as display stands and supports for making shelf units or as stimulus material.
Wood, brick and stone effect wallboard, wood, brick and stone effect papers	Use as backdrops for displays or covering materials for display stands.
Coloured emulsion paints	Use to upgrade old and unattractive pieces of furniture to be utilised as display units (e.g. old chairs, tables, desks).

SCRAP MATERIALS	POSSIBLE USE IN DISPLAY
Old or broken furniture	Break up and reassemble as display units for three-dimensional work.
Boxes, cardboard tubes, plastic bottles and tubs, offcuts of wood, matchboxes, cotton reels, wool, raffia, old tights, pieces of ribbon, card and polystyrene packaging, discarded items from shop window displays, discarded advertising material	Most waste or scrap materials can be used in a variety of ways, for example as display stands, holders for display labels, or for creating effects (cobwebs, underwater scenes, space scenes, cave scenes). Display felt can be used for covering boxes or large cardboard cutout figures. Shop window dummies can be dressed in uniforms, period costumes, or as story characters.

MISCELLANEOUS MATERIALS	POSSIBLE USE IN DISPLAY
Cane furniture, cushions, beanbags, vases, urns, flower-boxes, mats and rugs, posters, pictures and prints, clip-on spotlights	Use to create welcoming and attractive displays in the entrance hall, foyer, reading corner, library, corridor, landing, or corner displays throughout the school.

Local traders

Local businesses and traders may also be a source of useful display material for little or no cost. The following suggestions are a guide.

Paper mills
Ends of rolls (newsprint), corrugated card, packaging, paper sacks, quality card and paper.

Printing works
Offcuts of various types and qualities of card and paper.

Supermarkets
Boxes, packaging, advertising materials.

Departmental stores
Display felt and other window display materials, display dummies, boxes, packaging.

Builders merchants
Chipped bricks and building blocks, offcuts of timber, sawdust, pallets, pipes, tiles, sheet materials.

Fabric stores
Remnants, ends of rolls, pattern books.

Home decorating/DIY stores
Wallpaper sample books, discontinued emulsion paint, offcuts of timber, damaged goods of various kinds.

Confectioners
Surplus sweet jars (for storage), tins, advertising material.

Scrap yards/car breakers
Machine or engine parts, wheels, pieces of trim.

Jumble sales, boot sales, junk shops
Picture frames, interesting bric-a-brac, unusual objects, stuffed animals and birds.

Potters
Seconds, vases, pots, sculptural forms.

Effective classroom display depends on teachers' ingenuity in the way they use and adapt the materials available to them. No source of supply should be overlooked — explore every possibility.

Logs and slices of tree-trunk make excellent display stands for objects in environmental displays. Logs cut at a 45° slant require a small piece of beading tacked across the surface to prevent slipping.

Children enjoy the unusual in a display.

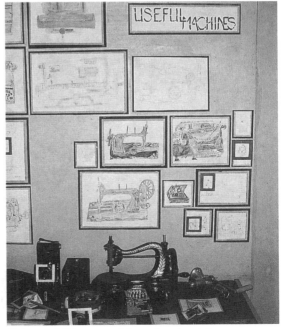

Using real things provides a focal point.

Stimulus Displays

An important, if not essential, feature of any classroom is the stimulus display. This is set up by the teacher to motivate the class and initiate interest in a new topic, project or programme of work. To begin with this kind of display is almost totally dependent on the teacher, although children may, of course, be encouraged to contribute items of interest to

An interesting stimulus display helps to raise the quality of children's work.

the display. For the display to be successful and to achieve the desired aim, you need to think very carefully about what material to include in order to promote the right level of curiosity and questioning. The display will most certainly form the starting point for the work in which the children will be engaged, covering most, if not all, of the curriculum areas. Over a period of time, which varies according to the nature of the display, the initial stimulus will give way to one that is dominated by the children's work, but this does not mean that the initial starting points should not remain until the conclusion of the topic or project.

A well-considered stimulus display is a powerful communicating force, not unlike successful advertising in many respects. Advertising is essentially about communicating a message, capturing interest and prompting action to buy a product. Good classroom display is similar. If the stimulus display is imaginatively presented and conveys carefully-selected information via exhibits, words, and pictorial images, it is likely to captivate children's interest and enthuse them to produce thoughtful work of quality.

Elaborate displays

Stimulus displays may take many forms, ranging from something quite simple to the complex and very elaborate but all may be equally thought-provoking and visually exciting. I know of schools where, because of falling rolls, vacant classrooms have been devoted to elaborate stimulus displays used to initiate a project or topic being followed throughout the school. Classrooms have been transformed

into space capsules, desert islands, castles, Victorian homes, witches' covens, and many other wonderfully stimulating environments. It quickly becomes apparent how well children are motivated by placing them in such imaginative and visually exciting environments and how this is reflected in the quality of the work they produce.

Corner displays

More commonly it is the corner of an individual classroom that is developed as a stimulus area, depicting a particular theme or topic that is to be researched by the class. One central feature can be the focus of the display with everything else relating to it. A full-size skeleton, borrowed from the School Museum Service, formed the centrepiece for a stimulus display on 'Ourselves' in one Kent primary school. The children were fascinated by this addition to their classroom and produced a whole range of work from observational drawings, fabric collage, batik, poetry, creative writing, and various mathematical investigations as well as the more obvious science and biological work related to it.

In another school, a Victorian living-room was created in the assembly hall. This display inspired each class in the school to develop a Victorian corner depicting aspects of Victorian life including home, work, school, toys, costume, and furniture. Again the children produced work covering most of the curriculum areas. Sensitive drawings and pieces of written work related to the numerous artefacts to be found around the school aroused interest and curiosity.

SUGGESTIONS FOR STIMULUS DISPLAYS

The following are suggestions of possible items for inclusion in stimulus displays for a wide range of topics and themes frequently undertaken in schools:

Seaside

Collections of shells, pebbles, driftwood; examples of dried and mounted seaweed; fishing nets, lobster baskets, floats; fish skeletons (borrowed from the School Museum Service); model ships, ships in bottles; sand, coral; small rowing boat; sailboard, surfboard, wet suit. Pictures or photographs of seabirds, boats and ships (past and present), lighthouses, fish and sea creatures, shells, seaweed and seaside flora. Maps of shipping routes and past sea voyages.

Public services

Large (life size) cutout figures of policeman, fireman, postman, etc; tailor's dummy dressed in borrowed policeman's, fireman's or nurse's uniform; borrowed helmets, caps, truncheon, stethoscope, breathing masks, X-ray plates. Examples of fingerprints. Model police cars and motorcycles, ambulance, fire engine. Pictures, photographs and posters of police cars, motorcycles, fire engines, and ambulances, road signs, aspects of safety, postage stamps, police dogs.

Houses and buildings

Examples of bricks, tiles, slates, pipes, building blocks, flashing, chimney-pots; examples of building tools (e.g. trowel, plumb line, float, surveyor's tape). Dolls' house and model houses. Models of building plant (e.g. bulldozer, dumper truck, earth mover, crane). Estate agents' photographs. Pictures and photographs of houses (past and present), building sites. Machinery, doors, windows. Architects' plans and drawings.

A possible stimulus display for a topic on 'Houses and Homes' — a cardboard house in relief with either model or 'stand up' drawn furniture for each room. Related written work and information could be mounted in class books.

Colour

Large cutout cardboard rainbow; examples of everyday objects grouped in colours (or arranged for the children to sort (e.g. toys, household items, buttons); examples of patchwork, ribbons, balls of wool, reels of cotton; items in jars (e.g. powder paint, water coloured with Brusho colour, inks or dye); samples of paper, fabric; sheets of coloured acetate (for 'colour mixing' on an overhead projector); paint colour charts; Rubic cube; vase of flowers; cutout cardboard artist's palette with colours depicted; balloons, prisms, kaleidoscope, colour wheels.

Wildlife

Live exhibits — when the circumstances are correct for keeping them. Stuffed animals, birds or reptiles (these can often be borrowed from the school museum service or even a local museum with prior negotiation). Animal skeletons, skulls and bones — often available, cleaned and hygenic, from an abattoir; feathers, skins, horns, antlers, teeth, tusks. Plaster casts of animal footprints. Incubator with chicken or duck eggs. Pictures and photographs of animals, birds, reptiles.

The human body

Human skeleton — borrowed from the School Museum Service, nearby secondary school or local hospital. Examples of bones and joints. Medical models of the eye, ear, brain. Large cutout cardboard figures with features labelled. Vertical measure for children to record their height and scales for children to record their weight. Display of baby photographs for children to identify each other. Display of photographs showing children at different ages; similarly for adults. Fingerprints, handprints, footprints. Pictures and photographs of children of other nationalities to show comparative features (e.g. Japanese, Chinese, Indian, West Indian, African, Mexican).

Simple ideas are often the most effective.

A possible stimulus display on the theme of light. The lighthouse and mobile pieces should be cut from thick card to add relief.

Machines, tools and bygones

Examples of old domestic machines (e.g. sewing machine, copper, mangle, bellows, flatiron, toasting fork). These can often be borrowed from local museums or the School Museum Service. Examples of agricultural implements (e.g milking equipment, seed drills, butter pats, cheese moulds, traps, butter maker). Items of historical interest (e.g. gas mask, Davy lamp, radios, television sets. Machine parts (e.g. gear boxes, engines, clocks, musical boxes, typewriter. Pictures and photographs of 'bygone' machines, industrial machines, factory assembly lines, robots. Working models. Large cutout cardboard cog wheels.

Light

Large cutout cardboard sun, moon and stars; large cutout cardboard lighthouse. Examples of light sources (e.g. bulbs, candles, oil lamp, torch, lantern, spot light, fluorescent tube, night light. Pictures and photographs of various light sources: Christmas lights, advertising lights, flood lights, search lights, Davy lamp, Olympic flame, dentist and operating theatre lights, disco lights, laser beams, flashing lights (police, fire, ambulance), street lights, lighthouse, light ship, road work warning lights. Batteries, plugs, generators. Pictures and photographs of sunsets, sunrises, night sky, beacons.

Looking at plants

Structure

Observational Studies

Colts-foot

We planted beans in different soil samples

Soil investigations

We collected some clay soil from the building site.

We mixed it with water and moulded clay pots.

We can see exactly how beans grow

The structure of soil.

Clay soil

beans planted in different positio[n] What happens?

Sources

Many of the items suggested may be borrowed from the School Museum Service in those authorities where such a service exists. The following alternative sources could also be approached with a view to borrowing material for classroom displays on a short term basis. With increasing contact being made between schools and industry and other places of work, requests of the kind suggested are likely to be met favourably. Bear in mind that you will generally have to be prepared to collect and return the borrowed materials.

Stimulus display material can possibly be borrowed from: local museums, police and fire stations, hospitals, department stores, farms, factories, workshops, builders, churches and other places of worship, shopkeepers, craft studios, and even the abattoir!

In some instances the 'lenders' may be

A visually exciting classroom provides a wealth of learning experiences for children.

prepared to come into school to talk about the borrowed objects and, where appropriate, demonstrate how they are made or used. This, combined with the stimulus display set up in the classroom, provides the almost perfect introduction for a new project or programme of work.

Seasonal and Thematic Displays

Almost all schools encounter times when displays of a special nature are required — celebrations to mark the major festivals of the year such as Harvest, Christmas, Easter, Mother's Day, Diwali, Ramadan, Pesach (Passover); or particular events such as Hallowe'en, Guy Fawkes' Day, school anniversaries, sports day, school visits and fund-raising activities.

Seasonal displays can create particular problems for teachers if they feel under pressure to avoid repetition and to produce a different look to their display each year. On my frequent visits to schools at festival times, I never cease to be surprised by the versatility of some teachers in producing original and visually exciting displays each year. While the basic content and theme of the displays remain the same, the approach and presentation vary considerably.

Often two-and three-dimensional displays are combined with a tabletop display, display board and hanging displays with a common theme. Stimulus material may be either natural or man-made, and work produced by the children frequently represents more than one curriculum area.

Such displays require a great deal of planning, whether by a teacher considering an individual display for the classroom or by the whole staff meeting to discuss a coordinated display theme to be developed throughout the whole school. This may include consideration of not just the content of the display but also the colour scheme, style of lettering to be used, and the positioning of each of the composite elements making up the total display.

Some schools prefer to concentrate special displays of this kind in the school assembly hall so that work can be presented on a much larger scale and be seen by the whole school population. This helps to create a corporate feeling about the display which is important because often all the classes in the school have contributed to it.

Collecting the right resources is clearly the key to most displays of this kind, and having a resource collection of display material as described in the chapter 'A Whole School Policy for Display,' saves time searching anew for items required on each occasion a seasonal display occurs.

Useful display resources

The following is a list of some of the resources found from experience to be useful in seasonal displays, and therefore recommended as items for schools to collect as part of their display resources. It may be felt necessary to have more than one of some of the items.

Hallowe'en

Besom broom; small bottles or jars containing coloured liquids and a variety of dried seeds to represent potions; large, round container to represent a cauldron; wooden spoons; decorated loose-leaf file to represent a 'Book of Potions' (children can then write their own recipes to go in the book); black pointed hat; black cloak; (an old academic gown is useful if it can be found); an old pair of black pointed shoes; bones and animal skulls; cutout moon and star shapes; snakes, bats and spiders can be made by the children.

Harvest

Willow baskets; trugs; watering can; gourds; house plants; examples of various seeds in transparent containers; dried flowers; garden tools; agricultural implements; cartwheel if it can be found (or borrowed); scarecrow; straw bales; artificial fruit and vegetables; fish if they are of good quality and look authentic (cheap, unrealistic versions should not be used); slices of tree-trunk; sacks; apple boxes; farm worker's smock; horse brasses; horse shoes; milk churn; beehive; honeycomb. (Fresh fruit, vegetables and flowers, sheaves of wheat, hop bines, baked bread, etc, naturally have to be provided each year.)

Simple 'bolt together' batten structure, cardboard panels for back and sides, cardboard roof covered with pine needles and other evergreens. Stores flat when dismantled. Can be built to any scale but most effective when made to house large Nativity figurines.

Christmas
Selection of decorations (e.g. baubles, snowflakes, wooden decorated figures); hoops; natural materials such as fir cones, tree bark; nativity figures (ceramic or wooden purchased or made by the children in clay or paper sculpture); straw bales; coloured candles; coloured ribbons; polystyrene scraps for building relief features; lanterns; decorated gift boxes; take-apart structure for creating stable scenes.

Easter
Willow baskets; decorated eggs (papier-mâché); palm crosses; Jewish artefacts (scrolls, seven-branched candlestick, goblets, clay wine bottles, pitcher, prayer shawl, skull cap — many of these items can be borrowed from resource centres, museums, or local Jewish communities). Bread and wine; Easter eggs, simnel cake, hot cross buns and other customary Easter foods will have to be provided each year.

Passover feast
It is often possible to use a stimulus display of relevant material as the focal point for development in other ways in the classroom. I have, on occasions, observed teachers 'dressed up' in traditional authentic costume, sharing a Passover meal with children in a classroom as a means of increasing their understanding of Jewish custom.

Other festivals
Displays for other festivals, including those of all the major world religions, can usually be resourced by contacting representatives of the appropriate religious community, who will often loan items of symbolic relevance and which are used in a celebratory way.

Victorian schoolday celebration
In a similar way, a collection of old school memorabilia including slates and slate pencils, maps and charts, inkwells, dip pens, examples of text books, copy books, certificates, registers, log books, uniforms, furniture (if it is available or can be borrowed), could form a fascinating stimulus display for a Victorian schoolday celebration to coincide with a school anniversary. (The display could, of course, be matched to any historical period as appropriate.) Children and staff, dressed in period costume, can experience together a typical schoolday of the times. A well resourced display of the kind described can act as a backcloth for much of the preparation and follow up work to such an event.

Cross curricular links

Thematic stimulus displays could well form the focus for developments leading to a whole range of activities in the classroom aimed at enriching the learning experience for children and embracing a number of curriculum areas. Examples of such developments might include a medieval banquet, evacuation party, Coronation Street party, Dickensian Christmas, Christmas customs around the world, or overseas themes.

Selecting materials

Many seasonal and thematic displays rely upon the careful selection of materials, as well as ideas and arrangment, for their success. Thought given to this aspect of the display can greatly increase its visual appeal. The introduction of tree bark, pieces of wood, pine cones and needles, straw, raffia, sand and evergreens into a three-dimensional nativity display gives it a certain authenticity. Similarly, dark shredded fabric, frayed string, cotton wool that has been 'teased', dangling threads, luminous paints and papers, dried leaves, berries and hips add atmosphere and charm to a Hallowe'en display. Stones, moss, sand, and soil may form the basis of an Easter garden. Leaves of all colours, shapes and sizes, twigs, seeds and fruits, bark and dried flowers may contribute the necessary additions to raise the quality of a harvest or autumn display.

Adapting the classroom

Earlier in the book I have referred to displays where a corner of the classroom is completely given over to establishing a particular environment that is linked to ongoing work in the class: a cave perhaps, or a newspaper reporter's office. I have been privileged on a number of occasions to see schools where 'environments' of one kind or another have been created throughout the whole building, much to the credit of staff, pupils, parents and friends. One of these was an infant 'jungle' classroom with hanging foliage, paper flowers, cutout animals, birds and butterflies. 'Christmas Night' was created in a school hall with rooftops and chimneys, reindeeer and sleigh, and Father Christmas with sacks of toys. The display was built on a large scale and contributed to by the whole school community. It served as a background for Christmas assemblies, carol concerts, parties and a Christmas fair — not to mention the inspiration it provided for written and pictorial work throughout the school.

Displays on this scale may not be within the scope of all teachers, but I would like to emphasise the benefits to be derived from an adventurous approach to display work generally.

Display and Presentation of Children's Written Work

The main reason for displaying children's written work is so that they can have the opportunity to read each others' efforts. Arranging work, however attractively, on wall mounted display boards requires careful consideration and presents a number of problems for the teacher:

1. Children's writing tends to be rather small and this makes it difficult to read at a distance when displayed on a vertical display board.

2. Display boards are often fitted at an unsuitable height, making it difficult for children to read work displayed on them.

3. Many children find great difficulty in reading work displayed on a vertical surface. Focusing on straight lines of small writing requires much concentration and considerable skill in scanning.

4. Children require time to read and comprehend lengthy pieces of written work. Unfortunately the most convenient times for children to read written work on display often correspond with those times when the classroom or other parts of the school have to be empty because of supervision or organisation difficulties, thus putting into question the value of displaying written work in this way.

5. To collectively display numerous pieces of written work in the confined space of a display board is generally unsatisfactory for the observer as it appears overwhelming and fails to sustain interest.

Alternative ways of displaying written work that are generally more attractive and stimulating will be considered later in the chapter, but there are situations and occasions when there is little or no alternative to displaying written work on vertical display boards, and it is most important to think about the way in which the work is arranged.

The following illustrations show a variety of arrangements for displaying the same pieces of work within a given space, first with regular and then irregular-sized pieces of work.

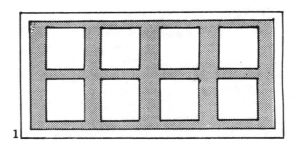

1

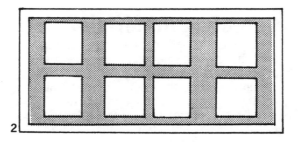

2

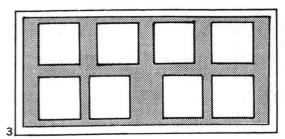

3

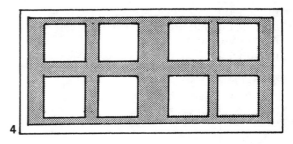

4

Regular-sized pieces of work

Figures 1-4 show different arrangements and groupings of the same pieces of work. Note the importance of careful spacing.

Figure 5 shows how the addition of a different heading leads the eye to a particular piece of work.

Figure 6 shows how importance is given to a piece of work in a display by using a different form of mounting.

The background colour on which work is mounted is also important. Bright colours can be distracting, but a contrast is certainly required.

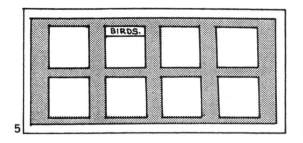

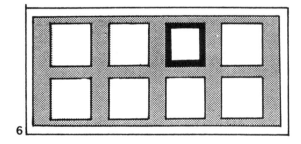

Irregular-sized pieces of work

Irregular-sized pieces of work are always more difficult to arrange and require careful spacing. Aim for balance between the pieces of work and the spaces. Dividing the background up in different ways can help to achieve a good balance.

Figures 7-10 suggest ways of displaying irregular-sized pieces of work to best effect. Note the variations in spacing, sequencing, and treatment of the background.

Figure 7 shows the five irregular-sized pieces of work arranged in descending order of size, leaving sufficient space for a heading.

Figures 8 and 9 show the display board divided into three equal sections with parts of the background treated differently from the others.

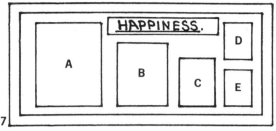

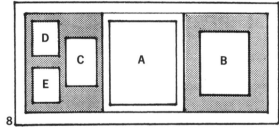

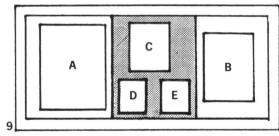

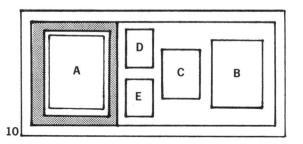

Figure 10 shows how emphasis can be given to one piece of work (A) by treating it differently from the remaining pieces.

Class books

Instead of restricting written work to a child's exercise book it is ofen more rewarding to display it in a class book, which makes it accessible to a wider audience. One of the main functions of creative writing is the sharing of ideas and thoughts, and a class book that can be hung in the classroom, corridor or entrance hall increases accessibility to the work and adds greater purpose to writing. You can make the book attractive and interesting with decorated covers, or shape them to convey the content of the book.

All the covers illustrated are made from folded pieces of card with the pages either stitched or stapled inside. They are all based on a rectangular shape.

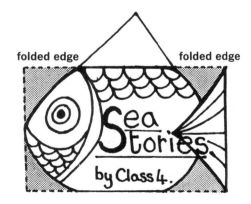

The shaded areas are cut away to provide the shape.

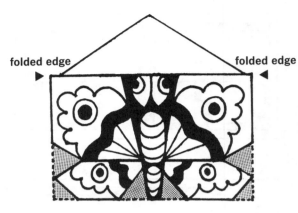

More elaborate class books can be made by adding details to the basic rectangular shape and decorating the inside pages with attractive borders and illustrations. This will be dealt with in a later chapter.

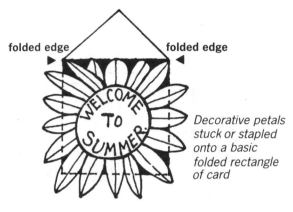

Decorative petals stuck or stapled onto a basic folded rectangle of card

shaded areas cut away

A butterfly collage cover made from pieces of decorative fabric or coloured papers. With distinct shapes such as this wording on the cover is often unnecessary; children will be enticed to look inside because of the colourful and interestingly-shaped cover of the book.

Class books made on this scale can be used by teachers reading to the class or by individual children reading each others' work.

Flames cut from thin polystyrene, painted and stuck onto a basic folded rectangle of card to give a three-dimensional effect

Story cards

Another way of making children's work available to a wide range of readers is to mount it — or write it directly — onto either single or double sheet story cards. These can then be used as part of either a class or school library. Collections of story cards can be exchanged between classes. Older children may be encouraged to write for younger ones. One class may become 'authors' and write stories or poems for the benefit of another.

Card made so that the written work is revealed through the open door (i.e. cut lines a-c, b-d, and c-d; score line a-b.)

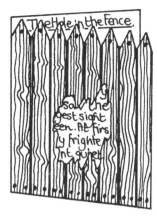

Here the written work is seen through the hole in the fence.

Story cards of this kind can be stored in cut down cardboard boxes that have been attractively covered or decorated. It is helpful for storage and cataloguing purposes if the cards are kept to a standard size, e.g. folded A4.

folded edge ▶

Card cut out into a window shape

Story or poetry cards made from folded card

These are ideal for short pieces of either poetry, or prose work. The cards can be used as supplementary reading material and may well stimulate written work in other classes.

Other suitable titles for 'hole' cards might be a ship's porthole, mousehole, manhole, prison bars, etc.

Story or poetry cards made from a single sheet of card or thick paper

Written work can be imaginatively presented by either mounting it or writing it directly onto sheets of card or thick paper (A4 or A5 size) that have been previously prepared in a variety of ways.

Faint illustrations, using coloured pencils, watercolours, or drawing inks can be created as backgrounds for pieces of written work. The work is seen to best advantage if either black ink or black fibre tipped pens are used.

Decorative patterns using a wax resist technique make interesting and colourful backgrounds for written work. Part of the design is made using wax crayons or candles. Brush this over with any water-based colour (e.g. paint, drawing inks, Brusho colour). Light colours or pale shades should be used to enable the writing to remain clear when it is placed on the top of the design.

An extension of this technique is to begin as described above but then to rewax additional areas of the design on top of the first layer of watercolour. This traps or seals some of the first colour used under the second application of wax. The design can then be brushed with a second colour of water-based paint, ink or dye. This process can be repeated many times, each additional coating of wax trapping some of the preceding layer of watercolour beneath it.

It is necessary to mount the written work onto this kind of background as the wax content makes it impossible to write directly onto the surface.

Another alternative method is to use coloured gummed paper or coloured tissue paper. Pasted onto a piece of backing paper this has the advantage of allowing work to be

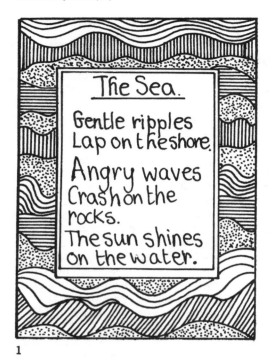

The Sea.

Gentle ripples
Lap on the shore.
Angry waves
Crash on the
rocks.
The sun shines
on the water.

1

HOPPING IN KENT.

It is 1931. My family and
I are preparing to leave
our home in London to
travel to Kent to go
hop picking. We shall
live in a small hut.
The work is hard but the
money is good. I love
the smell of the wet
hops, the bonfires burning
and the food cooking.

2

clouds floating across

a sun filled

winters sky. Light

grey wisps of softness

racing across the world

4

3

Bubbles.

Bubbles floating, light as
air. Transparent
sculptures of every colour.
Rising, falling. Fading.

written directly onto the prepared surface. It is
often effective if the writing follows the line of
the pattern. If gummed paper is used, cut
edges are usually more successful, whereas
with tissue paper torn edges produce interesting
results.

Pieces of torn tissue can be pasted in
overlapping layers onto a piece of backing
paper using a weak mix of wallpaper paste. It
is most satisfactory if the paste is applied both
under and over the tissue. When the
background is dry and the writing has been
completed the whole surface can be lightly
brushed with a coating of diluted PVA adhesive,
which acts as a varnish to seal the work and
give it an attractive sheen.

1. Wax resist technique is ideal for a background of
   waves and seashore.

2. A painted or crayoned background to a story
   card.

3. Overlapping layers of tissue paper make the
   background of this effective bubble picture.

4. Here gummed paper has been cut into the
   shape of clouds.

A concertina book with a Christmas theme

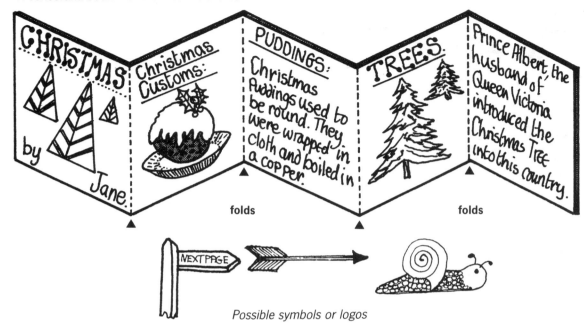

folds   **folds**

Possible symbols or logos

Story boards

As an alternative to class books story boards are an interesting way of grouping stories together for display purposes and use in the classroom. Cut pieces of stiff card so that they can be held together at the base by a paper fastener through holes punched in each piece of card. Work can then be mounted on both sides. The illustration shows a simple chopping board shape, which makes it easy for children to look through and select a story or poem of their choice to read, thus encouraging them to write for a wide readership.

Groups of four to six stories make easy-to-handle story boards for classroom or school library use.

► **Punched hole and paper fastener fixing**

The cards can be decorated with a background design or border to make them more attractive and eye-catching.

Zigzag or concertina books

These can be quickly and easily made from thick, folded sugar or cartridge paper. The advantages of this type of story card is that it can be opened out and seen as a whole if displayed flat on a horizontal display surface; be stood up on end, concertina fashion, on a horizontal display surface, which makes for easy viewing; or present written work and illustration side by side, enabling the work to be followed sequentially.

A simple symbol or logo placed in an appropriate position on each page will ensure the book is folded and read in the correct order.

Concertina books can be made as short or long as necessary. Additional sections can be easily joined using either a suitable adhesive (Pritt stick, PVA, etc) or double-sided vinyl tape. Different sections of the book can be identified with different coloured papers.

This kind of book is particularly suitable for stories that have a 'chapter' structure to them, or work that naturally breaks down into sections or phases. The Christmas Story, historical events, log books, diaries and anthologies based on themes that have an obvious sequence to them (e.g. an alphabet of animals, the seasons, the weather) are ideal subjects.

shaded areas cut away

shaded areas cut away

Cards that have been folded along the top edge can be displayed by hanging them on a stretched curtain wire or even a taut piece of string.

Cards folded this way can be displayed free standing on horizontal display surfaces or stored in cut-down boxes as described and illustrated under 'Story and Poetry Cards.'

Work written on single cutout shapes. These could be decorated in the same way as story cards.

Cutout shapes

Children work best when they are interested in what they are doing and are motivated. Many children find being faced day after day with lined paper a daunting prospect, but they do find great satisfaction in seeing their written work closely related to work achieved in other areas of the curriculum in which they have had success. This clearly adds purpose and credibility to their writing.

It is often quite simple ideas that capture a child's imagination — such as writing within shapes that convey something of the content of the writing. This is often sufficient to increase interest in the task, sustain concentration, and raise the quality of their work.

Single cutouts can be collectively mounted in a class book, or alternatively be presented as individual shapes cards.

The shapes chosen should not be too complex but they must be large enough to

Cards can be kept in a simple pocket holder made from two pieces of thick card. A wide piece forms the back and a narrow strip is taped and stapled onto the front. If you use coloured vinyl tape it gives an attractive border effect. Make the pockets by spacing strips of double-sided vinyl tape at appropriate intervals between the back of the narrow strip and the front of the wide strip of the card, or by using staples. The pocket holder can then be attached to a wall-mounted display board.

enable the writing to be contained on one side of the paper if it is to be mounted in a class book.

Similar pieces of work mounted on backing paper or frieze paper could be used to form a story or poetry frieze.

It is important that displays of this type are changed regularly in order to sustain interest and prevent the work from becoming dog-eared. This is, in fact, a general principle applicable to all good display.

Relief pictures and dioramas

Written work will frequently be linked with work carried out in other areas of the curriculum, particularly art and craft. If the various aspects of the work are eventually brought together to form a display value is immediately given to the work and its purpose is enhanced.

Children greatly enjoy making three-dimensional scenes depicting the content of a piece of written work, and it offers the ideal opportunity for language work to be seen in relation to other forms of creative expression.

The following illustrations show how children's written work and aspects of art and craft can be brought together to provide stimulating and visually exciting displays.

Relief pictures

Relief pictures can be made quite simply from a flat sheet of card, scored and folded to make two side flaps. The finished work can be either free standing or displayed on a vertical display board. Mount the written work on the two side flaps, leaving the centre panel for an illustration of the text. Prepare a background so that the cutout image can be mounted on to it in relief. The image may be decorated in contrast to the background or left as a silhouette cut from black card. The image can be mounted on a matchbox sleeve or a folded cardboard hinge to provide the 'relief' effect.

Diorama

A three-dimensional scene can be made in a cardboard box that has been attractively decorated.

The two side flaps can be used as panels for mounting the written work. Cut the top and bottom flaps of the box to provide a border that frames the scene inside the box. Make the images from cut and decorated card and then stick them onto the box with a small tab, using either adhesive or double-sided vinyl tape. Similar scenes can be made in boxes that have been cut away to a much greater extent. In this way written work can be mounted on the back of the box so that it can be read above the scene depicted. All of these ideas are appropriate for original creative writing or the retelling of familiar or traditional stories.

A relief picture made from a flat sheet of card.

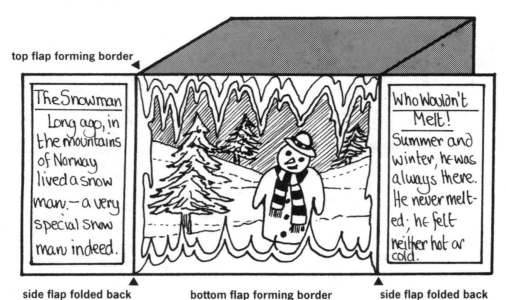

top flap forming border

The Snowman

Long ago, in the mountains of Norway lived a snow man. — a very special snow man indeed.

Who Wouldn't Melt!

Summer and winter, he was always there. He never melt- ed; he felt neither hot or cold.

side flap folded back　　**bottom flap forming border**　　**side flap folded back**

A three-dimensional diorama made in a cardboard box. The snowman and trees stand up on folded tabs.

tab scored and folded

HOLIDAY ADVENTURE.

At last! The holidays had started. The journey was behind us and we were soon on the beach. It

didn't take long to discover the rock pools and caves. Imagine our surprise when we found a small wooden

chest. Where had it come from? Who did it belong to? As we sat thinking things over we heard strange

noises from the back of the cave. Filled with fear we ran from the cave to watch from a distance......

If required additional written work can be displayed by hanging it from the front edge of the diorama.

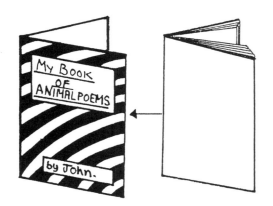

Simple card cover and paper insert book made by folding, stitching or stapling.

Handmade books

Finally we must not forget the pleasure children get from making their own books. This brings together a wide range of skills, including creative writing, illustration, calligraphy and lettering, design and layout, as well as bookbinding. Handmade books offer scope for both individuality and originality. Children should be encouraged to think carefully about the relationship between the text and the supporting illustrations, as well as the quality of the layout and the general presentation.

Handmade books may be simply folded pieces of paper held inside a folded card cover by staples, or something rather more substantial and complex with board covers, bookcloth spine, and decorated cover and endpapers. Whichever is considered most suitable, the children will get great satisfaction from presenting their work in such an attractive form. The following illustrations and notes provide guidance for making handmade books.

Cover and end paper decoration

WAX RESIST
The cover and endpaper decorations may be done with either candle or coloured wax crayon directly onto the card cover and brushed over with water-based paint, ink or brusho colour. The wax resists the liquid wash, allowing it to colour only the unwaxed areas.

PAPER BATIK
This is a development of wax resist, completed in stages. Start in the same way as for wax resist by making a pattern or design directly on to the card cover using either a candle or coloured wax crayon followed by a wash of light-coloured water-based paint, ink, or brusho colour applied with a brush. When dry, rewax parts of the pattern on top of the first brushing of water-colour, trapping some of the colour under the second application of wax. Then brush the whole design with a second, slightly darker wash of water-based colour. This process can be repeated as many times as necessary to obtain the number of colours required. Remember to allow drying time between each subsequent washing and waxing.

PASTE-COMBED PATTERNS
Another effective way of making book cover designs is to paste-comb them. Mix powder paint with cellular wallpaper paste to make a creamy consistency. Then brush the whole of the card cover with this coloured paste. Fascinating patterns can be made in the wet paste by using fingers (finger-painting) or a simple 'comb' cut from stiff card.

You can get an even more attractive result by drawing a design on to the card cover with either wax crayons or coloured chalk before it is brushed with the coloured paste. This allows the colours of the wax or chalk to come through the pattern made in the wet paste. When the paste is completely dry it can be brushed with diluted PVA adhesive or lightly polished with wax furniture polish to seal the pattern and give it a slight sheen.

WET PAPER COVERS
Paper that has been soaked in water receives colour in a very different way from dry paper. Inks and brusho colour in particular, brushed or 'dropped' onto wet paper, produce interesting blends and effects. The results are even more fascinating if the paper is screwed up before it is soaked. Open the paper out carefully after soaking. When the colour is applied it floods into the many creases and folds, creating delightful effects.

Alternatively fold the paper into a regular shape and dip it into containers of coloured ink or brusho colour. The ink will seep into the paper and produce an uneven distribution of colour in varying degrees of density.

MARBLING
Marbling is a traditional craft used by bookbinders for decorating endpapers of books. Interesting results can be achieved with the simplest of materials and equipment. Children enjoy experimenting with marbling techniques and it gives them a small insight into the bookbinder's craft.

You require a deep-sided tray, half-filled with water. Drop oil-based marbling inks into the surface of the water in random blobs. These can then be broken up and swirled together using a marbling comb or feather to produce marble-like patterns.

You can make a simple comb by driving oval nails or panel pins through a batten of wood. The nails or pins should be equally

A comb made from stiff card

Marbling comb made from wooden batten and nails

spaced between 5 mm and 10 mm apart. By pulling the comb through the tray of water, the oil-based inks will be drawn into exciting and colourful swirling patterns.

Drop cartridge or similar weight paper onto the surface of the water, and the pattern made by the oil-based inks will be transferred onto the paper. Tap the surface of the paper while it is floating on the water to release any air bubbles trapped underneath. If this is not done, unattractive white blotches will appear as gaps in the surface of the patterned paper.

After a few seconds lift the paper from the surface of the water, allow to drain and lay out to dry. As the surface of the water is constantly moving, so the pattern made by the inks changes, producing slightly different results each time.

If the inks do not appear to adhere to the paper very well, the addition of a little wallpaper size or cellular paste to the water before dropping the inks may help.

These ideas for making book covers are some of those most frequently used and enjoyed by children (and teachers!). You might also like to try various kinds of printed covers using potato or linocuts, polystyrene, card or string. You could also use paper-backed hessian, padded fabric, drawn illustrations or cut paper collage.

Stiff covered books

Making stiff covered books involves the children in the whole range of skills associated with book production.

THE COVERBOARDS
Glue cardboard cover boards to a piece of bookcloth (linson or buckram), leaving a small gap (5 mm) between the boards to take the pages of the book at a later stage. Cut the book cloth larger than the cover boards to allow for the ends to be turned over and glued to the inside of the coverboards. (Figures 1 and 2).

DECORATIVE COVER AND END PAPERS
You now need decorative cover and endpapers, of the kind previously described. Stick the cover papers onto the cover boards, taking care to leave an equal amount of bookcloth showing along the spine on both the front and back of the book (Figure 3). The cover papers need to be cut larger than the cover boards to allow for an overlap at the front, top, and bottom edges. The corners need to be cut away (mitred) slightly proud of the corners of the cover boards to ensure a neat joint on the inside of the book. (Figures 4 and 5).

THE PAGES
Make the pages of the book from folded paper cut to a size slightly smaller than the overall dimension of the joined cover boards.

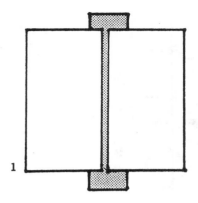

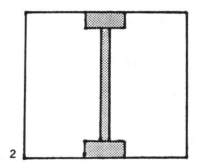

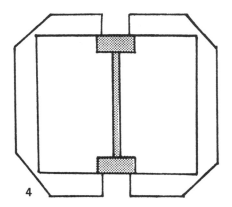

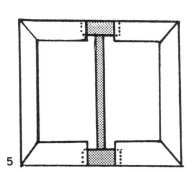

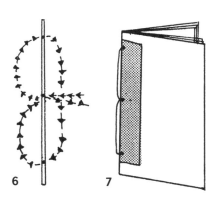

The pages can be made up from a selection of papers so that white pages are interspersed with coloured ones. Thought needs to be given to the number of pages that will form the inside of the book, as children find it difficult to stitch through too great a thickness of paper. Stitch the pages using a simple figure of eight stitch. (Figure 6). Complete the stitching by tying a firm knot on the inside of the pages so that they cannot move or slip. The outside page should be the decorated endpaper, which should be stitched with the decorated side facing inwards.

Finally, stick a piece of bookbinders' muslin or bandage down the back of the spine of the book. This reinforces the book and stops the needle-holes enlarging, causing the pages to become loose in the cover. (Figure 7).

ASSEMBLING THE BOOK
The final stage of the process involves bringing together the cover boards and the pages. The pages are held in the cover by the endpapers.

It is a good idea to insert a piece of scrap paper between the front endpaper and the remaining pages to prevent adhesive being smeared on them. Spread diluted PVA adhesive over the whole endpaper, including both the underneath and top of the bookbinders' muslin.

After removing the scrap paper, line the spine of the page section up in the gap between the cover boards and the endpaper smoothed down onto the front cover board. Repeat the whole process with the back endpaper and cover board.

The use of decorative borders, variations of layout, and styles of lettering will be considered in a later chapter.

Illustration showing the pages stitched with the decorative endpapers facing inwards.

Assembled book, showing the front endpaper stuck to the front coverboard, fixing the pages firmly into the cover.

Borders, Edges and Decorative Features

Just as a frame helps the eye to focus on the composition of a painting, so do decorative borders and edges draw attention to a display of work. In this chapter we will look at the effect of decorative borders, edges, and other features on the presentation of children's individual pieces of work and display of a more general nature in schools and classrooms.

It is a good idea to show children examples of page layouts from a variety of different texts so that they can see how printers, designers, and illustrators use borders and other forms of decoration to break up areas of text and improve visual appearance and impact.

Victorian texts, illustrated diaries, log books, and manuscripts all make good reference material. Your local library or the school library service would almost certainly help to identify suitable material.

It is clearly helpful if a school policy on display and presentation exists. If children are taught from an early age to think carefully about the quality of presentation of their work, including making use of decorative borders, by the time they reach upper junior level they will be able to produce work that holds together in every respect — where content, layout, and other aspects of general presentation all command attention and contribute to the overall level of achievement.

A display resource bank

Each display needs to be considered individually at the planning stage. Sometimes a simple symmetrical arrangement is all that is required to show work to best effect, while at the same time clearly conveying the intended meaning

Examples of page decoration will help to inspire children to enhance their own work.

of the display. At other times the display may require a more complex approach that will add impact and attract much greater attention.

With this in mind, it is helpful to make simple preparatory sketches of the layout of proposed displays and, if possible, photographs of the finished product. These can then be kept as a record of displays and in turn become a valuable and time-saving resource for future reference. An instamatic or polaroid camera is therefore a useful addition to a school's resources. If the whole staff contribute to such

a collection it is surprising how quickly a display resource bank can be built up and this will become a well-used facility in any staffroom.

Alternatively, if classroom and general school displays are photographed in slide form a number of schools could contribute material to a collection held at a teachers' or professional development centre. Such a collection could then be loaned out to individual teachers or to a whole school staff to be used at an in-service curriculum development or school policy workshop.

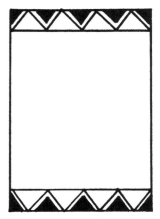

Border at top and bottom of page

Border at one side and bottom of page

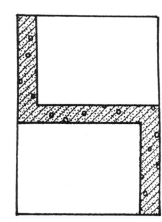

Border used to divide page into equal divisions

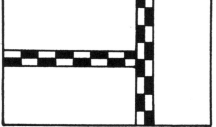
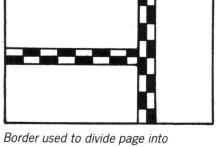

Border used to divide page into irregular divisions

Border at both sides of page

Pictorial and non-pictorial borders

These illustrations show a variety of ways in which decorative borders can be used to improve the visual appearance of individual pieces of work.

Border across middle of page

Border on two sides and bottom of page

Border on all four sides of page

Using decorative features

Sometimes it is not appropriate to border or edge a piece of work completely — for example when this would break the flow of the work, or cause confusion to the reader. Clearly the purpose of a decorative border is to enhance the written work, not to dominate it. An alternative is to use decorative features to complement the text.

Children should be encouraged to think of a piece of work as a whole so that the written work and illustration are considered together. It is possible to introduce an element of fun into the illustrations, as some of the examples show. The prime function, however, remains the same: the illustrations exist to support the text. Simplicity is frequently the key to successful illustration. The amount required will vary according to the nature of the work, but often a little is better than too much.

The following examples show a variety of ways of using decorative features to add interest to children's writing in a number of different areas of the curriculum.

Feature placed in random arrangement

Feature placed in diagonal corners

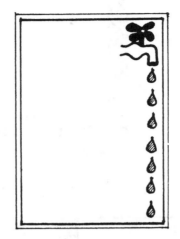

Feature placed down one edge

Feature placed in a 'trail' arrangement

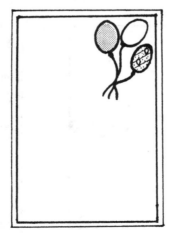

Feature placed in one corner

Feature placed in each corner

Feature radiating from one corner

Wall displays

In the same way that decorative borders enhance the visual appearance and layout of individual pieces of work, so they can do much to improve the effect of wall displays. The inclusion of some kind of border or edging around a display helps to focus the eyes on the main content.

The type of border will vary according to the nature of the display. For displays that consist mostly of regularly-shaped pieces of mounted work it is unlikely that anything more than a piece of straight card edging would be required to 'frame' the display. If the display board is already set in a wooden or aluminium frame, as many are, then probably nothing more will be needed to help the eyes 'read' the display.

More complex displays, particularly those of a composite nature, are much more effective if a border is used as an integral part of the overall display. This often gives the display a three-dimensional appearance, even though the border may only be raised out slightly from the display board. If it is possible to raise the border from the surface of the display board some of the features of the display can be arranged to appear as if they emerge from the border. This leads the eyes into the display. In

Raised borders can be fixed to display boards by drawing pins.

order to achieve this parts of the border can be mounted onto cardboard tabs, the sleeves of matchboxes, or long narrow boxes such as toothpaste boxes that have had the ends cut off.

The following illustrations show a variety of ways of creating imaginative borders using a range of easily obtainable materials.

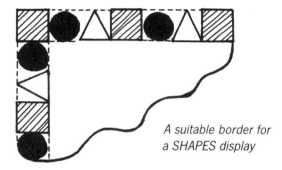

A suitable border for a SHAPES display

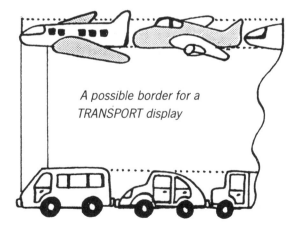

A possible border for a TRANSPORT display

Borders like this could be made from long continuous strips of card. Or they could be made up from individual pieces of work brought together to form a border around a display.

They could also be used for other purposes. For teachers working with young children they can become the basis of simple mathematical games:

How many shapes can you count?
How many triangles are there?
How many blue squares are there?
Are there more cars than lorries?
How many wheels can you count?

By using displays in this way children become familiar from an early age with the idea that displays are a valuable and interesting learning resource within the classroom. They learn to sharpen their powers of observation and come to expect that their learning environment will always have something different and exciting for them.

Concertinas

A visual environment that changes frequently will gain the children's attention and command a response from them. However, with the increasing pressures on teachers' time it is important to consider time-saving methods of achieving the desired results.

By using the concertina method, long strips of identical images can be produced very quickly, providing an ideal way of making borders for display boards.

Linking a common theme

Borders can be used to form links with other areas of a display to create a common theme. For example, a WEATHER display may use sun and cloud symbols as material for making a border around a display board. The same symbols may then be used around the edge of a table that provides a horizontal display surface. Display stands, used to raise the level

Paper folded concertina style

◀ **shaded areas cut out**

The cut figures are joined by the hands and feet.

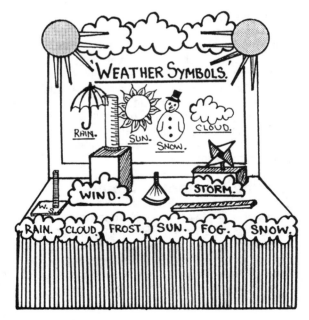

An example of a silhouette border

of particular exhibits, may also carry the same symbols so as to create a degree of uniformity within the whole display.

Silhouettes

Silhouettes make very striking borders. The images need to be very clearly defined. The absence of colour helps to focus attention on the central features of the display. Black cutouts mounted on a white background are the most effective, but coloured images can be successful, particularly if the colour relates to the theme of the display.

Materials

Polystyrene in tile and sheet form — or the packaging from hi-fi equipment, television sets and washing machines — is a useful material for making borders and edges to frame displays. It is particularly useful for showing the link between one view and another within a display (e.g. the outside and inside of a building, above and below ground level).

Polystyrene is reasonably easy to cut with either a sharp knife, fine bladed hacksaw or a hot wire cutter. The following examples show

display boards framed with borders made from polystyrene and cardboard.

It is possible to incorporate natural materials into displays. The choice generally has to be restricted to materials that will not wilt or droop too quickly. Ideal examples are small branches or twigs to simulate trees in winter; or wheat and barley to bring interest to a harvest display.

Care needs to be taken in fixing such materials to display boards. Whereas most borders and edging materials can be held in position with double-sided vinyl tape, double-sided adhesive pads, or staples, natural materials can be more of a problem. The easiest and neatest way of fixing them is by wiring them onto small screw eyes inserted into the frame of the display board.

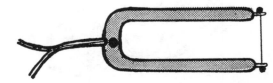

Simple battery-operated hot wire cutter, suitable for cutting polystyrene.

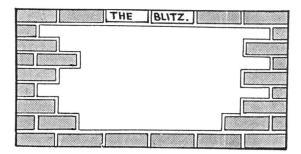

Brick border made from polystyrene, enabling the viewer to look into the building. Brick effect wallpaper could also be used.

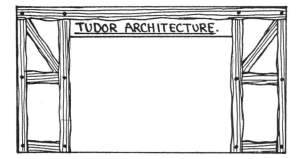

Timber frame border made from sheet card, with raised timbers made from cut polystyrene. Aspects of both the outside and inside of such a building are displayed together.

Possible subjects

Finally, here are some more examples of possible borders for classroom displays. They cover a range of curriculum areas and topics frequently used by teachers working with primary school pupils, and it is likely that the children themselves could contribute to them all. These are only random suggestions: you will think of many others and the children themselves will have their own ideas. As mentioned earlier, it is a good idea to keep a record as a future reminder.

Borders could easily be provided for displays on the following topics: animals, birds, building, colour, communication, farms, fire, flight, holidays, ourselves, public services, seashore, seasons, time.

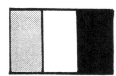 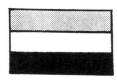  

FLAGS: Suitable for displays on the EEC; imports and exports; specific countries.

SHIELDS: Suitable for displays on heraldry; knights; armour; battles; castles.

MODES OF TRANSPORT: Suitable for displays on inventions; history of transport.

BUILDINGS: Suitable for displays on architecture; local study; street trail; homes.

Booklets, Worksheets and Programmes

Most schools regularly produce booklets, worksheets, and programmes for a wide range of class and school activities and there are many ways of making these varied and attractive in design, layout, and visual appeal. Your school probably has a photocopier or facilities to reproduce original work by ink or spirit duplicator. A4 paper is generally used for producing this kind of material, and there are various methods of presentation that the children could be encouraged to try out.

When different ways of folding are tried out, the 'master' will need very careful preparation. Some of these suggested formats will require more than one 'master' (either a spirit duplicator master or an ink duplicator stencil.) You will need to work out the layout of the master so that when the copies are folded after duplicating the content of the worksheet or programme comes in the right place and can be read sequentially. It may take more than one attempt to master this, but the effort is well worth it for the imaginative and visually exciting results. If children are going to be involved in the planning of duplicated worksheets, it is best if they make up a 'dummy' so that they can work on the balance between text and illustration, general layout and visual appearance. Photocopying makes the whole process much quicker and easier, but it is, of course, a very much more expensive method.

Design and layout

The design of worksheets and programmes can be approached in the same way, but booklets generally pose different problems and will therefore be dealt with separately.

When designing a worksheet the following points need to be considered:

1. Has enough information been provided?

2. Is the layout clear and logical to follow?

3. Are the children going to work directly on the worksheet? If so, is there enough room for them to write or draw their answers?

4. Does the design and layout provide for a range of interpretation or is it 'tightly ordered', giving only limited space for written responses and pre-drawn boxes that will condition the size and scale of drawings?

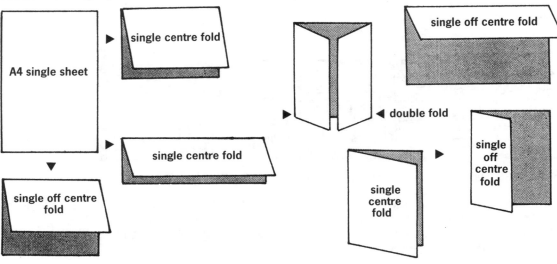

A4 single sheet
single centre fold
single centre fold
single off centre fold
single centre fold
double fold
single off centre fold
single off centre fold
single centre fold

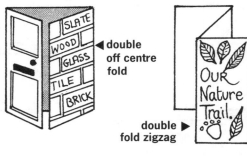

double off centre fold

double fold zigzag

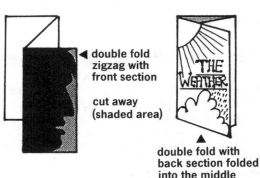

double fold zigzag with front section

cut away (shaded area)

double fold with back section folded into the middle

5. Is the worksheet visually attractive and therefore more likely to interest the children over a sustained period of time?

6. Does it enable the children to find out and learn what was intended?

7. Does the design of the worksheet (e.g. the quality of calligraphy and illustration) encourage children to take pride in the level of presentation?

Worksheets that contain only vast quantities of written matter are off-putting to most children and consequently fail to motivate them. Illustration is therefore important as it breaks up the text visually and provides a different focus of interest. It can also help children to interpret the text more easily. A particularly effective use of illustration is to lead the children from one part of a worksheet to another. This can be achieved in a number of ways:

1. Making an illustration wrap around a fold or section of worksheet and completing it on a different part.

An example of a wrap-around illustration.

2. Repeating a symbol or motif in different places on the same worksheet.

3. Using the same symbols or motifs across a range of worksheets having a common theme.

4. Changing the position of the illustration on different parts of the worksheet to keep interest alive.

5. Providing an equal balance between illustration and writing as a means of developing both observational and imaginative drawing with written recording or expression.

Duplicating original material

If the children are simply making their own individual worksheets or 'folded booklets' the illustrations can be drawn directly onto the paper. But if a child's drawing is to be duplicated for a supply of worksheets sufficient for a whole class then a number of processes can be considered, which will depend on the combination of reprographic equipment available. Most reprographic requirements can be catered for with a combination of the following: a spirit duplicator; an ink duplicator; a thermal heat copier; a photocopier. A computer with a printer can also be a useful addition.

There are various ways of reproducing either children's or teachers' original illustrations or commercially produced work in order to obtain multiple copies. Some methods appear to be more complex than others, but they enable the work of very young children, who would otherwise be unable to cope with some of the alternative processes, to be used.

Drawing directly onto ink duplicator stencils or spirit duplicator masters

Both these methods can be used by teachers, but very few primary-aged children would have the skill required to cut an ink duplicator stencil with a stylus. Similarly, drawing directly onto a spirit duplicator master, used in conjunction with a carbon, requires some expertise because mistakes are not easy to erase. Photocopying is the best way to reproduce direct drawing, but this is an expensive way of producing multiple copies.

Using a thermal heat copier in conjunction with an ink and spirit duplicator

Heat copiers can be used for a number of functions ranging from laminating workcards and making overhead projector transparencies to transferring original or commercially-produced illustrations (or written text) directly onto specially manufactured ink duplicator stencils or spirit duplicator masters in readiness for duplication. The original illustration is fed into the heat copier together with one of the appropriate stencils or masters.

The ready-prepared stencil or master can then be placed onto the relevant duplicator and the required number of copies run off. This is a comparatively cheap method of obtaining large numbers of good quality copies that can then be coloured by the children to make them more attractive and appealing.

In addition to producing worksheets, programmes, and school journey and visit booklets, some schools make their own Christmas cards, invitations to school celebrations and events, posters, notices, car stickers, badges and other display materials using this method.

Enlarging

Few children are able to enlarge original drawings free hand. Encourage the child to trace the original drawing onto a piece of

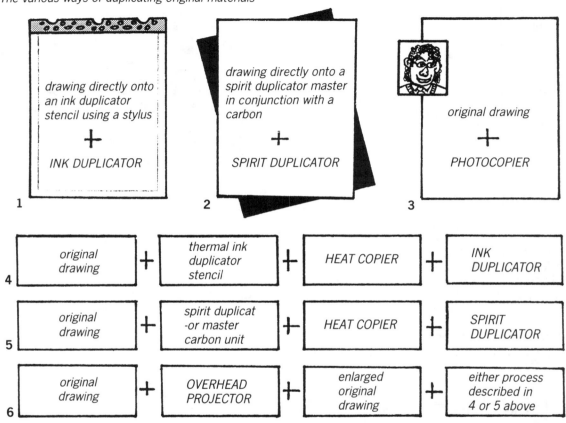

The various ways of duplicating original materials

1. drawing directly onto an ink duplicator stencil using a stylus + INK DUPLICATOR

2. drawing directly onto a spirit duplicator master in conjunction with a carbon + SPIRIT DUPLICATOR

3. original drawing + PHOTOCOPIER

4. original drawing + thermal ink duplicator stencil + HEAT COPIER + INK DUPLICATOR

5. original drawing + spirit duplicat-or master carbon unit + HEAT COPIER + SPIRIT DUPLICATOR

6. original drawing + OVERHEAD PROJECTOR + enlarged original drawing + either process described in 4 or 5 above

Copyright regulations must be observed when reproducing published material.

acetate and using an overhead projector, project the image onto a piece of paper fixed to the wall with Blu-Tack. The drawing can then be retraced and, in its enlarged form, used in the processes previously described. The best reproductions will be obtained if the originals are drawn with a soft grade pencil (2b/3b) or Indian ink.

Booklets

Reproducing booklets for school visits or local studies projects can be a problem because the stencils or masters have to be typed in such a way that the pages are in the correct order when they are assembled and stapled. Assuming the size of the booklet to be folded is A4, you need a long carriage typewriter so that two pages can be typed onto each stencil or master.

To avoid placing the contents in the wrong order it is always wise to make up a dummy booklet. This will not only ensure the correct sequence of pages, but also provide an opportunity to plan the arrangement of illustrations. Because of the way the stencil or master has to be typed (or written), it is essential that the whole booklet is planned and the layout decided at the same time, otherwise the spacing and continuity is likely to become confused.

Take as an example a booklet made up from eight pieces of folded A4. The numbering of pages, and therefore the sequence in which they need to be typed, are as follows:

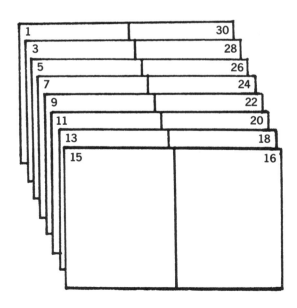

Pages 1 and 30 are on the reverse of the front and back cover. The paired numbers on the reverse side of the arranged sheets are as follows:

2 and 29	10 and 21
4 and 27	12 and 19
6 and 25	14 and 17
8 and 23	

This method of sequencing is not required if the booklet is to be held together in either a plastic spine binder or a spiral binder. In this instance the pages would run in the order: 1 and 2, 3 and 4, 5 and 6, etc.

Children become involved in producing booklets for a wide range of uses. These may include publications to be sold as part of the school's fund-raising efforts. I have known schools who have produced their own anthology, or a group of schools who have combined to compile a group anthology. Others have produced a children's cook book containing a collection of favourite recipes, news bulletins, school magazines, quiz and joke books, and booklets for special occasions such as twenty-fifth or fiftieth anniversary celebrations. All of these ideas are ideal for the inclusion of children's written and illustrative work.

Booklets can be considerably enhanced by giving a little extra thought to the design and presentation. Using different coloured duplicating papers for each section of a booklet makes identification of the sections very much easier and quicker. Similarly, different coloured papers can be used for work representing different classes or age groups. Colour coordinated booklets can be visually most attractive and eye-catching. Different tones of the same colour used for the cover and the pages respectively is often very successful (e.g. dark blue cover with light blue pages).

Alternatively, alternating the colour of the pages creates interesting variety (e.g. green and white, blue and white, green and yellow, etc).

In some booklets, such as anthologies, each new section can be preceded by a title page illustrated by children's drawings that introduce the theme of the work that is to follow. In a school cook book children could design their own symbols to head each section (e.g. meat dishes, cakes and biscuits, desserts, quick snacks, etc). Some of the ideas included in the chapter on borders and edges might also be incorporated.

Spiral binding provides a neat presentation but requires a special machine for punching the holes.

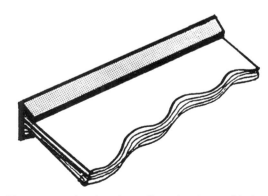

Plastic spine binders have the advantage of being inexpensive.

The cover

The cover is most important, as the initial impression generates interest. A child's illustration almost always captures interest, but it does require careful positioning and setting off by good, clear lettering. Use dry mount lettering such as letraset to make the ink duplicator stencil or spirit duplicator master; or cutout letters from newspaper headings can be a cheap way of producing clear lettering for reprographic work.

Headed notepaper

In one school in which I taught, as a means of motivating an interest in letter writing, I encouraged the children to design their own headed notepaper on which they could write thank-you letters or letters of request to friends of the school or representatives of the local community. This proved popular with the children and their efforts were much admired and appreciated by the recipients.

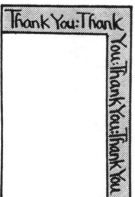 

Examples of headed notepaper.

Attractive work can be reproduced using a minimum of reprographic equipment. These examples were all produced from original drawings using duplicators, photocopiers and heat copiers. Line drawings can be attractively coloured using felt-tipped pens or coloured pencils. Note the different layouts and dimensions.

Such sheets can be designed by the children for various events that appear regularly in the school calendar such as harvest thanksgiving, celebrations for Christmas, sports day, open day evenings, school concerts and productions, class assemblies, school fairs and fêtes, book weeks, PTA dances, social events, educational talks and workshops, and other similar occasions.

The prepared and duplicated sheets may take the form of invitations to parents, governors, and other guests; or thank-you letters to speakers, visitors or local members of the community who may have helped the school in a particular way (e.g. school nurse, police liaison officer, charity representatives,

theatre companies, local clergy, etc). Alternatively, they may be simple gift or message cards to accompany items being sent out from the school to particular target groups in the community such as old people or handicapped children.

Whatever form the publication may take, presentation is most important as it is a means of conveying to the local community the value that is attached to high standards of work. Many of the publications that I have described also contain work by members of staff, governors, parents, and representatives from various sections of the community, and this is to be encouraged.

Lettering for Displays

When tutoring inservice display courses I receive more requests for assistance with lettering problems than almost any other aspect of display technique. Although many teachers show excellent skills in presenting imaginative and visually exciting displays, lettering continues to present problems and teachers constantly seek advice about how to produce lettering of an acceptable standard, which is at the same time visually attractive and eye-catching.

Good lettering skills are not learnt overnight! They require much time, effort and practice, which many teachers find difficult to build into their busy schedule. Modern materials have eased the situation to some extent as pleasing results can be obtained using little more than chisel and round-tipped felt and fibre pens

once the basics of 'stroke' and 'flow' have been mastered. However, there are other things to consider such as the scale of the lettering to be used, the selection of appropriate letter forms, correct spacing, and the choice of colour and texture of the letter forms — all of which add to the success or otherwise of the finished result.

Like so many aspects of good display, time taken in the preparatory stages produces quicker results in the long term. Whilst pens and brushes are essential tools for producing well-formed lettering, there are many other materials that can be used to achieve fascinating results, and reduce the need for skilled lettering. In this chapter I suggest a range of ideas for creating imaginative and eye-catching headings, captions, and labels.

Using an overhead projector

An overhead projector is a useful piece of equipment that can be used to assist teachers in a number of different ways. Examples of commercially-produced lettering can be traced onto acetate sheets (OHP transparencies) using spirit-based (permanent) overhead projector markers, which will prevent the finished sheets from being smudged. Capital and lower-case letters are best kept on separate sheets, or alternatively 'paired' on the same sheet (i.e. capital and lower-case letter next to each other) for quicker identification. The originals for tracing can come from various sources, for example newspapers and magazines. If the same source is used, the typeface remains consistent and over a period of time the whole alphabet can be accumulated. Fix sheets of paper to a wall with display putty (Blu-Tack) and project the cutout on to them, using the overhead projector. Headings, titles, and even sentences can be made up using the cutout letters.

The advantage of using an overhead projector is that the size of the letters can be adjusted by moving the projector nearer to or further away from the paper. Using this method, letters up to a metre high or more can be produced from an original tracing, on acetate, from a newspaper. Other sources of lettering suitable for tracing may be found in advertising material, catalogues, and packaging. Even letters traced from car number plates can be reduced or enlarged by projection.

I have involved groups of parents and older junior-aged children on this kind of activity during wet lunch hours, with great success and benefit to the school. The cutout letters can be kept in the staffroom or resource room in separate envelopes according to letter size and style, so that they are readily available for teachers to make their selection for the heading or title they require. The cutout letters can either be stuck on to a backing sheet or displayed individually using Blu-Tack, staples, or small pins to attach them to the display board. This is a very successful way of producing lettering, as styles appropriate for the age group being taught can be selected (e.g. lower-case infant script for reception aged children).

Using a thermal heatcopier

There are alternative ways of achieving the same results. One method is to make an overhead transparency from an original using a thermal heat copier. This will permanently 'fix' the copy of the original onto the acetate and eliminate the need for tracing. Printers' typeface samplers make excellent originals.

Templates

A slightly longer and more tedious method is to cut out letters from newspapers or similar sources and stick them onto cardboard to make them more durable. These can then be used as templates for drawing round (one of the few acceptable uses for templates) or for projecting as previously described.

Special effect papers

Any of the overhead projector methods will produce a range of results depending on the paper used. Plain, coloured papers are in many ways the most successful, although some particularly interesting results can be obtained by cutting the projected letters out of 'special effect' papers such as brick and stone wallpaper or model-maker's papers (suitable for topics on building); metallic papers for Christmas displays or a theme of reflections; or gift wrapping paper, which is now produced in a variety of designs ranging from patchwork and lace, grass and leaves, to baked beans and liquorice allsorts!

Three-dimensional lettering

Headings made from three-dimensional letter forms that stand out from the surface of a display board are always effective. Three-dimensional lettering can be produced in a number of ways using a variety of materials.

Cardboard cutout letters, decorated or covered in any appropriate material such as printed and woven fabric, felt, self-adhesive vinyl, decorative papers, wood veneer, or sandpaper can be mounted on small blocks of polystyrene and pinned onto a display board, raising them between one and two centimetres from the surface.

Letters can also be cut from vinyl floor tiles. Warm the tiles slightly before cutting, and when cool the letters become rigid and make

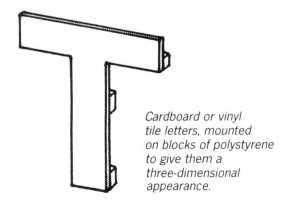

Cardboard or vinyl tile letters, mounted on blocks of polystyrene to give them a three-dimensional appearance.

excellent display headings. Either stick them onto a background, or punch holes in them so that they can be pinned in position and used over and over again.

Using a hot wire cutter

Using a hot wire cutter, three-dimensional letters can be cut from sheet polystyrene. Although the finished letters are quite fragile they make a striking impression, particularly if the white letters are mounted onto a black background.

Plasticine

Plasticine or similar modelling material can be used to produce 'fun' lettering. Roll the plasticine into coils and make the letters by simply shaping the coils. Alternatively the coiled letters can be slightly flattened and textured by pressing random objects into the flat surface. Press the finished letters lightly onto a textured background and pin them through into the display board.

Small holes should be made in clay letters prior to firing so that they can be pinned onto the display board.

Clay letters

Clay letters can also be formed from coils in a similar way. This can make a fascinating class project from which work in many other curriculum areas may develop. The clay letters can be textured or decorated and then glazed and fired. Clay letter headings can become attractive features around a school, identifying particular rooms or titles for permanent displays.

Tactile letters

Some of the leading educational suppliers supply tactile letters of various kinds that are intended to help children in letter recognition. They also make excellent letter forms for display headings, or they can be used as originals in conjunction with the overhead projection methods of producing lettering previously described. Most of the letters are made from plastic or vinyl and can therefore be stuck down with small tabs of double-sided vinyl tape.

Using scrap materials

Scrap materials can be used very effectively to make imaginative three-dimensional lettering. Objects such as bottle-tops, small coloured plastic lids, caps from the tubes of sweets or toothpaste, cotton reels, small blocks of wood, and a host of other odds and ends can be easily stuck onto a cardboard background using PVA adhesive. Using the kind of materials mentioned, even the more curved and difficult letter forms can be produced.

Novel ideas

An element of novelty is a sure way of capturing attention. In one classroom the heading for a display on the topic of 'People' was made with letters cut out from photographs and magazine pictures, pasted onto cardboard, of people — faces, fashion photographs, sports stars, pop stars, people at work, TV personalities, politicians and others. This idea could be applied to a whole range of other topics such as food, sport, houses and homes, transport, farms, animals. Make the letters by mounting the pictorial images onto cutouts of letters that are slightly larger, allowing for a plain margin of colour to be left around the edge.

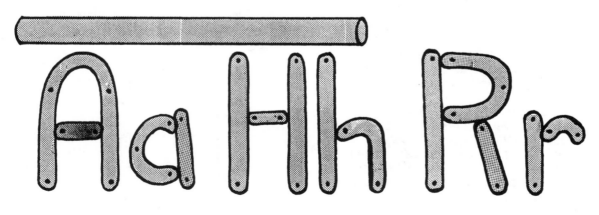

Letters formed from plasticine coils

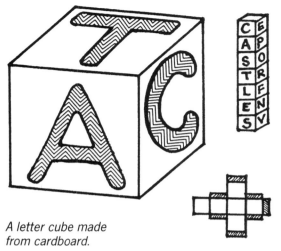

A letter cube made from cardboard.

Letter cubes
Another simple yet effective method of creating three-dimensional lettering for displays is letter cubes. Draw or cut out the letters and stick them on to the six faces of the cube. A series of cubes, each bearing an assortment of letters, can then be selected for making up headings and titles for displays. Letter cubes can either be pinned to display boards or used horizontally or vertically as free-standing arrangements for three-dimensional displays on table tops. With careful planning interesting colour combinations can be worked out.

Cuts and folds
Several interesting lettering effects can be obtained by simply scoring and folding paper or cardboard after the lettering has been completed. The following examples illustrate some of the possibilities, but it is well worth experimenting with different combinations of cuts and folds.

Forming corrugations in paper or card
Using a piece of thin cardboard (3-sheet thickness) or heavy quality cartridge paper, draw a display title in a style appropriate to the theme of the display. Fix the beginning of the title onto the display board and allow corrugations to form in the card as it is positioned. Each of the 'dipped' sections can be either pinned or stapled down, finally fixing the end of the title in the same way as the beginning.

Concertina folds in paper or card
Again, using either thick paper or thin card, write a display title on a flat strip in a suitable style and scale to be seen from a distance. When complete, score the strip and fold concertina style. Fix to the display board by pinning or stapling the dipped sections.

Scored and folded paper or card
This form of heading requires careful planning as it depends for its success on the letters

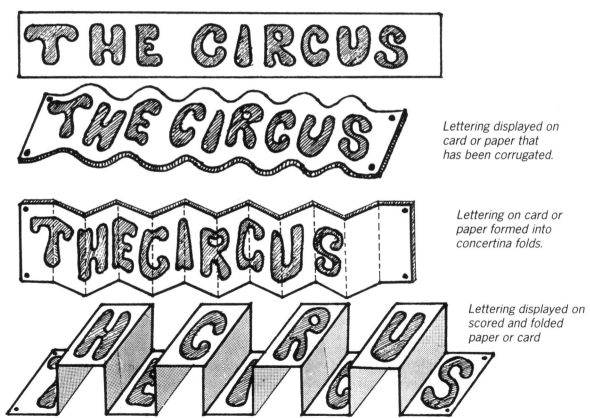

Lettering displayed on card or paper that has been corrugated.

Lettering on card or paper formed into concertina folds.

Lettering displayed on scored and folded paper or card

being accurately positioned on either high or low levels of the arrangement. An equal space needs to be left between each letter to allow for the folds that give the heading its depth. The sections left for the letters will need to vary in size according to the letter (e.g. 'W' taking more space than 'I').

Mounted letters

Titles and headings often need to be prominent, both in their composition and placement. Letters that are striking in their appearance and bold in scale are more likely to attract attention and be successful vehicles of communication. This can be achieved in a number of ways, as the following illustrations indicate.

Cutout letters on shaped mounts

Letters cut out from paper or card and mounted onto background shapes can be arranged in various ways. The shaped mounts can be made from scrap materials such as different shaped packaging that has first been painted or covered.

The mounted letters can be displayed directly on a vertical display board, or alternatively they can first be mounted onto a flat wooden batten and hung, in shop-sign fashion, slightly in front of an associated display. If the cutout letters have been mounted onto pieces of flat card rather than three-dimensional mounts, interesting effects can be achieved by partly overlapping the letters when they are arranged.

Similarly, titles and headings made up from letters arranged in shaped mounts, depicting the theme of the display, are almost always successful in their appeal to children.

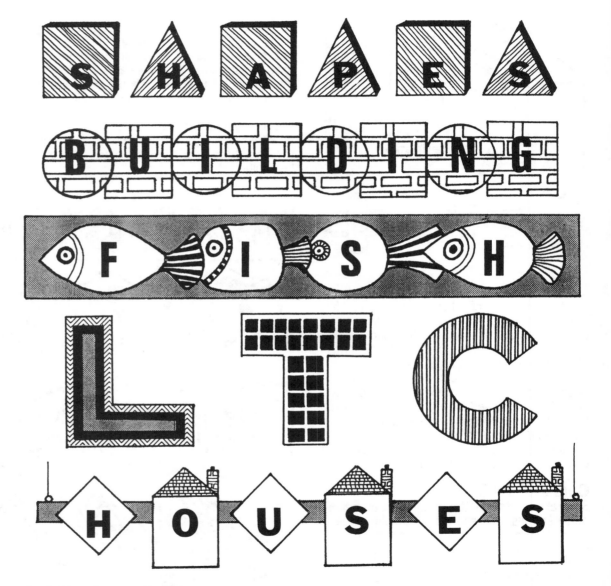

A selection of mounted letters.

Building up the surface

Cutout letters can also be enhanced by building up the surface of the letter to make a three-dimensional image. Layers of card, in different colours or tones, can be built up in contour fashion as illustrated by the letter 'L'. Mosaic letters are effective and can be easily produced by sticking small pieces of card onto the surface of the cutout letters, as illustrated by the letter 'T'. All kinds of materials, other than card, can be used to produce mosaic-type effects. These might include both manmade and natural items, such as pieces of ceramic tile, dried seeds, shells, vinyl floor tiles, pieces of carpet, or milk bottle tops.

Covering with textured materials

Letters can also be cut from or covered with textured materials such as corrugated card, as illustrated by the letter 'C', sandpaper, crumpled kitchen foil, felt and other fabrics.

Imaginative ideas from the children

Consideration should also be given to lettering of a more imaginative nature. Children frequently contribute ideas of their own for a style of lettering that emphasises the topic by its very design. In addition to providing interesting and usable display material, a design project of this kind is well within the scope of junior-aged pupils and often produces a whole range of ideas not thought of by the teacher. If the originals are produced on a small scale they can be transferred onto clear acetate, using an OHP pen, and enlarged onto paper or card by the methods previously described.

The following examples suggest scope available for imaginative designers, whether child or adult!

Whilst this style of lettering is initially more time consuming to produce, it is a further example of the kind of material that can be retained in a school display resource collection and made available to all members of staff. If the school policy encourages each teacher to add their individual creations to the school collection it is surprising how quickly a bank of imaginative and useful material accumulates.

Using natural and manmade materials

It is possible to produce very acceptable standards of lettering without having to master pen and brush strokes at all. Clear, eye-catching lettering can be made from a range of carefully selected natural and manmade materials.

In some cases you stick the material directly onto a background and mount it. Or hold the chosen material in place on a piece of background card using Blu-Tack, and then spray diffuser, or colour by applying paint, drawing ink or Brusho colour with a piece of sponge or a soft pad of cloth. Finally, remove the material to leave a clear, sharp image in the applied colour.

Materials suitable for forming letters might include drinking straws, rubber or vinyl piping, string, ribbon, buttons, small pieces of wood or plastic, twigs, feathers, shells, small pebbles, leaves, ferns, dried seeds.

With some of the more rigid materials (i.e. drinking straws, twigs, pieces of wood, etc) it may be necessary to form the rounded letters by cutting the material up into very small pieces. Or make the letters slightly angular in appearance.

Using fabric

Letters cut from felt or other fabric can be stitched or stuck onto a background in a bannerlike form. The use of fabric extends the range of lettering possibilities, but equally effective results can be achieved using paper and card.

Making shaped labels

Labelling a display helps to draw it together and convey its meaning clearly to the viewer. Well-scripted labels or captions always improve the appearance of a display but depend upon carefully developed lettering skills. It is possible to achieve attractive captions by using a more simple lettering style incorporated into cut-out illustrated shapes. Suitable designs to reinforce the theme of a display can be drawn on paper, duplicated on a photocopier, pasted onto card, and finally coloured. To add uniformity to a display the same shape can be used throughout with different words in each.

Examples of original designs can be kept in a folder for future use, or alternatively stocks of finished products can be placed in a school display resource bank and made available for all members of staff to use when developing a similar topic or theme. In this way time, effort and money can be saved.

Further examples of shaped labels may be found at the end of the book.

The fun element

Finally, I would suggest that lettering should sometimes contain an element of fun. It does not always have to be formal in appearance, using only traditional letter forms. The visual attraction of letters is often in the way they have been decorated, even though quite basic

Shaped caption cards

shapes may have been used. An endless range of techniques can be used to decorate letters, and some are described and illustrated here for your consideration.

Using lines

1. Change the direction of lines on different parts of the letter.

2. Change the thickness of lines on different parts of the letter.

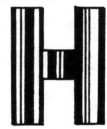

3. Use a variety of lines on different parts of the letter.

4. Use a variety of colours, tones or textures on different parts of the letter.

Wax resist decoration

1. Scribe random lines with a candle onto cutout letters. Brush over with water-based paint, Brusho colour, or drawing inks.

2. As above, but repeat the process in stages. Wax and apply colour, rewax (trapping some of the first colour under the second application of wax) and brush with a different colour.

3. Produce a design with coloured wax crayons, leaving parts of the background unwaxed. Brush over with water-based paints, Brusho colour, or drawing inks.

Wax scraper board

Cover cutout card letters with a layer of coloured wax crayon. On top of the first layer of wax, cover with a second layer of black wax crayon. Scape a design into the wax layers using modelling tools, dip pens, or other slightly blunted tools. This method of decoration lends itself to very detailed designs.

Instead of a single colour being used for the first layer of wax, stripes or patches in several colours will produce multi-coloured results when designs are scraped through the top layer of black wax.

Searching for inspiration

It is useful to scan all sources of 'public lettering' for ideas that can be adapted for classroom display use. Styles of lettering vary greatly, and often traditionally relate to particular trades or situations. Look at such sources as fairgrounds, amusement parks, arcades, markets, canal boats, shop and inn signs, gratings and grills, chainstores and supermarkets, church notice boards, billboards — and anywhere else where lettering plays an important part.

Interesting lettering should be regarded as an integral part of good display.

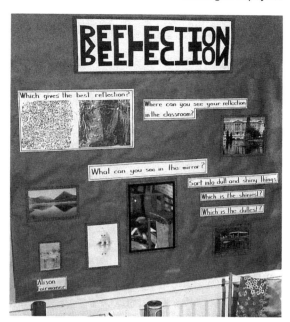

Hanging Displays

Lack of display space is a problem common to many schools. One way of solving the problem is to use the space above the children's heads. Displaying work at a high level is not ideal for children, whose eye level is very much lower, but when space in other places is limited imaginative and eye-catching results can be obtained from hanging displays.

Using pillars

With very little structural change, or expense, work can be hung at a convenient height from ceilings and beams, across corners, and on or between pillars. This is particularly useful in schools where there are large expanses of glass and not much wall space. Schools of this type are often of a girder frame construction,

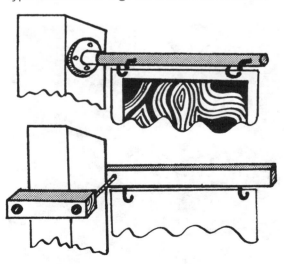

Battens attached to pillars

and as a result there are boxed in pillars in classrooms and other areas of the school. These can be adapted to provide useful support for creating additional display space.

Attach battens to the pillars by drilling, using a metal cutting bit, and screw wardrobe hanging rail holders to the pillar, into which dowels can be placed. Alternatively, sandwich the pillar between two lengths of batten (one long, one short) held tightly together by long bolts.

Screw small cuphooks into the battens — or use panel pins, nailed in at a slight angle. The size of the work to be displayed needs to

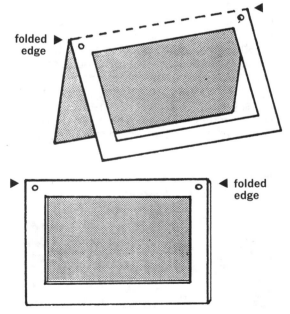

folded ▶
edge

◀ folded
edge

be standardised so that holes punched in the top line up accurately with the cuphooks.

Mount the work in cardboard window mounts to make sure that it hangs vertically. Although the mounts will initially be costly to produce in terms of both time and money, they can be used over and over again if made so that different work can be slipped in and out through one open end. Reinforce the punched holes in the top of the mount with a metal eyelet, using a combined punch and eyelet tool. This prevents the holes from tearing open, thus extending the life of the mounts.

Using the method described to fix battens to pillars, work can be displayed in a variety of ways:

1. Arranged down one side of the pillar.

2. Alternating between both sides of the pillar.

3. Arranged down both sides of the pillar.

It may be possible to span the space between two pillars, if they are conveniently positioned, and considerably increase the display space. This is particularly useful for hanging large scale pieces of work such as class pictures or friezes. Alternatively, fix the batten between window frames, where these are made from wood, but take care not to obstruct opening windows or block too much light from entering the room. Work can then occupy some of the window space, which means that an area generally considered difficult for display has been utilised, with the added bonus that the work can be seen from both inside and outside the school.

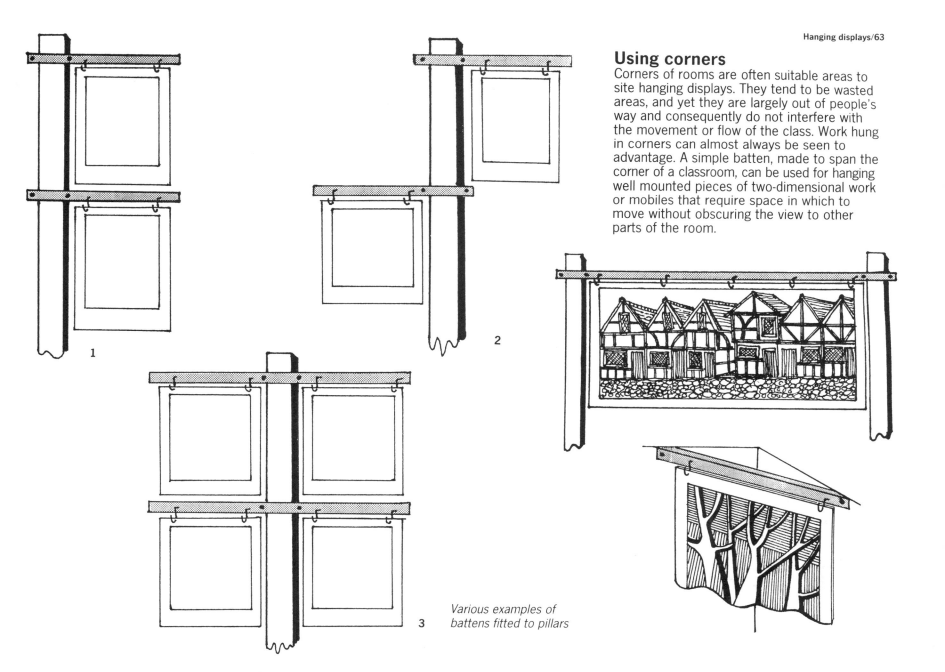

Using corners

Corners of rooms are often suitable areas to site hanging displays. They tend to be wasted areas, and yet they are largely out of people's way and consequently do not interfere with the movement or flow of the class. Work hung in corners can almost always be seen to advantage. A simple batten, made to span the corner of a classroom, can be used for hanging well mounted pieces of two-dimensional work or mobiles that require space in which to move without obscuring the view to other parts of the room.

1

2

3

Various examples of battens fitted to pillars

Using the ceiling

In very lofty classrooms it is sometimes possible to hang work in a central position without it being a problem. Again, although the height at which the work is displayed is not ideal, the fact that it forms a central focus is sufficient for it to attract attention and feature as a major part of the overall display. Such a display can be easily achieved by suspending a simple square batten frame using either nylon fishing line or thin wire. Work for display can then be hung from each of the four sides if it is two-dimensional, or alternatively mobiles could be hung from each corner.

The work could be further enhanced by focusing some spotlights on to it. The clip-on variety, available from most DIY or chainstores, are very good value for money and can usually be positioned near to a power socket in most classrooms.

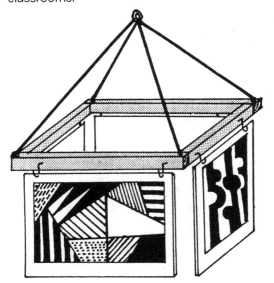

A simple square batten frame

Using garden trellis

In many classrooms garden trellis can be used effectively to create additional display space. The type sold in panels is particularly useful; it is not heavy and can therefore be hung from ceiling beams or other appropriate points that are able to take the weight. Hang the panels either parallel to the wall or at right angles to it. For more permanent use, fix the panels to the floor and walls. Shelves can then be fixed to the panel for displaying three-dimensional work, thus extending its usefulness.

Garden trellis is particularly useful for hanging or fixing at right angles to the wall between ceilings and worktops to create bays that can be developed for different curriculum areas, each one carrying a display appropriate to the activity being followed.

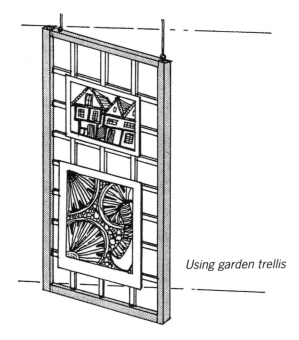

Using garden trellis

Inexpensive hanging methods

For schools with little wall space the facility to hang work is essential. The following two simple and effective ways of providing hanging displays can be achieved in almost any classroom situation. They involve very little cost and can easily be installed in appropriate positions.

Attach plastic poster hangers or spine binders to a suspended wooden batten using impact adhesive. This makes a very useful hanging facility for two-dimensional work, posters, charts, and maps. It may be necessary to edge the item for display with card at the top and bottom in order for it to 'grip' in the binder, and to slightly weight it to enable it to hang straight.

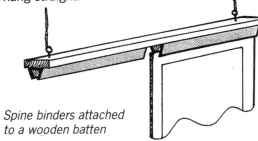

Spine binders attached to a wooden batten

Alternatively, cover a length of dowel with foam pipe insulation, using either PVA adhesive or double-sided vinyl tape. This method is adequate for hanging lightweight work using dress-making pins or mapping pins. The foam insulation could be painted with emulsion paint or bound with strips of crepe paper to make it look less drab when there is no work hanging from it.

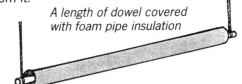

A length of dowel covered with foam pipe insulation

Mobiles

Mobiles can be used in a variety of ways to improve the visual environment of a classroom and to support work in a number of curriculum areas. They can often be made to relate directly to two-dimensional displays mounted on wallboards.

Mobiles do not have to be wholly pictorial in content as it is possible to use them effectively to reinforce vocabulary, introduce unfamiliar words, or provide word lists on selected themes. Useful themes might include weather symbols, faces, figures from the Bayeux Tapestry, two- and three-dimensional mathematical shapes, characters from stories or pantomimes, fish, leaves, fruits, birds, types of transport.

A number of children can contribute to the making of a mobile and its very movement when complete attracts attention and provides a sound learning situation.

Mobiles range from the very simple to the more complex. The following examples show a selection of mobiles in which pictures, words, and symbols have been used.

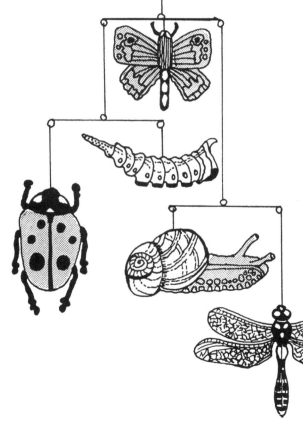

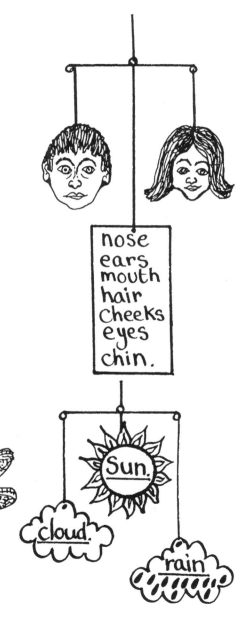

Some examples of mobiles

Multi-image mobiles

A simpler way of producing a multi-image mobile, avoiding the problems of balance, is to hang the component parts from a piece of crossed thin wooden batten. This permits the various parts of the mobile to be hung at different levels, from the ends of each of the four arms, from the halfway point on each of the arms, and from the centre — accounting for nine component parts if required.

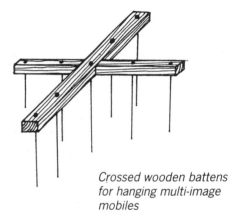

Crossed wooden battens for hanging multi-image mobiles

Linking different levels

It is sometimes necessary to give some thought to linking different aspects of a display. This often involves linking two-dimensional work displayed on a vertical wallboard with three-dimensional work arranged on a table or display block positioned in front of it. It is possible to link the two together using a 'relief' technique by attaching part of the display to the wallboard and then bringing it out to join with the three-dimensional display.

One group of teachers with whom I recently worked successfully achieved this in a display

This Hallowe'en display creates an impression of depth

on colour by arching a cutout cardboard rainbow from a wall display board onto a table in front of it that contained a display of books and other items intended to stimulate interest in and increase an understanding of colour. This display also successfully incorporated simple mobiles of coloured discs, each printed with the appropriate colour word hung in front of the two-dimensional display. Both this and the following display idea, tried by the same group of teachers, were achieved in the most dismal of mobile classrooms.

Creating an impression of depth

An impression of depth can be created by hanging cutout features a small distance in front of a two-dimensional wall display, thus providing a three-dimensional effect. This simple idea was successfully achieved in an impressive Hallowe'en display.

The intention was that children should imagine themselves to be looking out of their bedroom window into the night sky. The two-dimensional wall display consisted of various Hallowe'en images mounted on a dark background. A cutout cardboard window frame was then hung, using nylon fishing line, a short distance out from the display board so that the children actually viewed the display through the window. Various other items, including imaginary potions, spell recipes and ingredients, spiders made by the children, and various Hallowe'en books were displayed on a table beneath the window and completed the display.

Similar effects could be achieved by looking through other cutouts such as a castle arrow slit window, a ship's porthole, a jail window, a giant keyhole, a space capsule window, or a bird hide window.

Children greatly enjoy the unusual and the unexpected and so this kind of display is likely to increase the amount of attention that the children give to it.

Fabric hangings

Finally, consider the possibilities of using wall hangings as part displays. Children's individual pieces of fabric collage or pictures can often be brought together to form a collective hanging for a classroom, corridor, entrance, or assembly hall. Pieces of hessian or similar heavy-textured fabric make ideal backgrounds for fabric pictures. Some work, however, is

An example of a fabric hanging

visually more attractive if it is attached to a web of criss-crossed hessian strips rather than a full fabric background. Most fabric pictures are best hung by attaching them to a length of wooden dowel. Either turn the top of the fabric and make a channel to receive the dowel, or cut the top of the fabric in castellated cuts, giving it the appearance of a medieval banner. The addition of some tassels on the bottom of a hanging makes it look even more striking.

Banners and wall hangings can be an interesting feature of school display. They can be hung either flat against the wall or at 90° to the wall if space is minimal.

Exhibitions and Permanent Displays

Most schools have occasions when displays of a special kind are required to mark events such as a school visit or journey, a particular anniversary celebration, or a new initiative in the form of a school and industry link, a mini enterprise project, or a foreign exchange. On such occasions the school may be on view to the wider community, and quite clearly the work on display is to some extent a measure by which the school is judged. The amount of care and respect that goes into the mounting and arranging of the children's work is indicative of the whole school ethos.

This kind of exhibition is sometimes restricted to one area of the school such as the assembly hall or main entrance but at other times it may permeate the whole school, with each class presenting a display of work as a contribution to the overall exhibition.

A display evening

One large Kent village primary school known to me stages an annual Display Evening to which the whole village and neighbouring villages are invited. The school adopts a theme and develops a programme of work, culminating in a display. The headteacher writes, in a booklet to introduce the evening to visitors:

'Our display evening is the fourth of its kind. In general we aim not to fossilise our activities but the response and interest generated has encouraged us to see it as a valuable event for the school, families and the local community. We feel that it may have particular interest for colleagues in the secondary field, giving an opportunity to view the work of a whole primary

school. Visitors are requested to move around the school viewing the work of each class in chronological order so as to build up an understanding of how children's learning develops between the ages of five and eleven.'

The idea of a display evening arranged on these lines is both impressive and informative. Not only is the work imaginatively and caringly presented, but there is evidence that it is the product of teachers and children working together in complete harmony, with the total support of parents and the wider community.

Screens and stands

Where a display is centred in one area it is important to arrange the work so that viewers can circulate easily. This will, or course, largely depend upon the facilities available. More and more schools are now purchasing some form of commercial display system for staging exhibitions and displays. Whilst they are expensive, they can be added to as and when money becomes available and in this way, over a period of time, an extensive system can be built up. Most systems consist of attractively-covered pinboard made in interlocking units that can be assembled in numerous combinations to provide bays, double-sided viewing areas, and variations in height. (Most measure around 6 feet by 3 feet (183 cm × 91.5 cm).

It is possible to make interesting arrangements with only a few display units, but for a large-scale exhibition a larger number offers greater flexibility of layout. If it is not possible for a school to purchase a system of its own, often a consortium of neighbouring

schools can share the cost, purchase a system between them and each keep two or three units with the knowledge that, if more are required for a special display, they are available nearby. Alternatively it may be convenient for a teachers' centre to make the purchase and then loan the system to individual schools by a booking arrangement.

Temporary display boards

There are times in most schools when additional display space is required in classrooms and other areas of the school but not on a permanent basis. As a solution to this particular problem it is reasonably easy to locate lengths of 'L' section moulding on to walls in strategic positions so that temporary display boards can be slid into position as and when required. Sectional moulding of this kind, mounted above and below a window, means that window space can be temporarily converted to display space (assuming that reduced light can be tolerated). Long stretches of corridor wall can also house display boards of this kind.

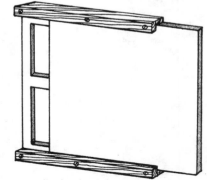

A temporary display board

Using staircases

In any exhibition the novel or unexpected is always likely to attract attention. Staircases are particularly good for displaying large scale work that lends itself to being displayed in sequence. Attach the work to the spindles of the staircase with wire twists such as those used for sealing freezer bags. The most suitable type of work for display of this kind is either large scale cutout work or panels that are designed to exactly fit the dimensions of the staircase.

Coping with large quantities of work

For most school exhibitions, such as open days or end of the year exhibitions of work, the major problem is often the sheer volume of work that needs to be displayed. White plastic curtain tracking, of the kind that has a perfectly flat front face, offers considerable potential for providing additional display space for exhibitions. With magnetic strip glued to the front face it is unobtrusive when not in use but, at comparatively low cost, can accommodate large quantities of work when required. The work to be displayed can be held on to the tracking by small tabs of magnetic strip placed over the top corners of the work.

In classrooms fitted with metal slatted Venetian blinds additional display space can be found by attaching work to the blinds using either magnetic strip if they are in the closed position, or small coloured plastic clothes pegs if they are in the open or semi-open position. Vertical blinds can also be adapted as additional display space in a similar way.

Work displayed on the staircase

Use of colour

Most exhibitions benefit from some sense of continuity and methodical sequencing that can often be achieved by adopting a system of colour coding for each section of the display. This could be represented in the colour of the background on which the work to be displayed is arranged, or in the mounts on which individual pieces of work are attached. Such a system enables the viewer to focus more easily on each section of the display and to follow the sequence. The colour coding may be organised to represent the work achieved by individual classes, year groupings, work completed in a particular term, or different aspects of the overall subject or theme of the display. Where different parts of a school are being used to stage an exhibition each area could use a different background colour for mounting the work to differentiate it from other parts of the display. Arrows, of the appropriate colour, could be used to direct the viewer from one part of the display to the next. An exhibition that is spread around a school building is often more successful than one concentrated in a single area. Mobility around the exhibition is made easier and interest tends to be heightened as viewers move from one part to the next.

Use of shapes

For special displays and exhibitions, where it is crucial to captivate interest, it is sometimes a good idea to move away from ordinary rectangular mounts and opt for other shapes that are more likely to attract attention. It may be possible to make a display arrangement from shapes that tessellate, such as hexagons, with each section bearing a different piece of information or example of work.

Alternatively, interesting arrangements can be made from combinations of shaped mounts that do not tessellate but that together form visually pleasing effects. Initially it will take quite some time to cut out and cover these mounts, but they can be kept as part of the school display resources and used whenever the occasion is suitable. Mounts can be cut

from thick card and covered with a choice of materials including paper-backed hessian, display felt, Vivelle, printed and woven fabrics, 'special effect' papers and even wood veneer (available in rolls from most DIY stores). This is another example of the kind of task that could be adopted by a group of parents as a PTA project to assist the school.

For further effect it is possible to introduce a three-dimensional element into the display by raising some of the shaped mounts from the display board. This can easily be achieved by first mounting the shape onto an open

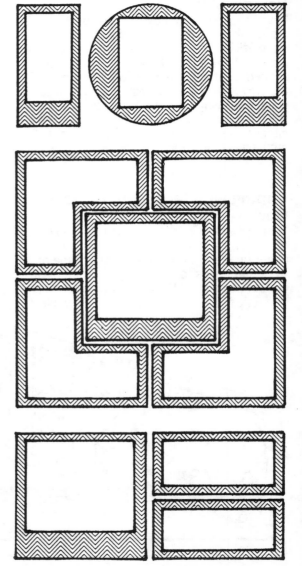

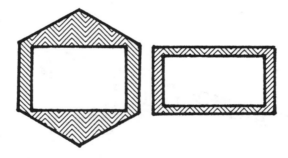

sleeve of folded and glued cardboard, which can then be pinned to the display board. Only a small number of shapes should be treated in this way so as to focus attention on key pieces of information or examples of work.

The following examples show different combinations of shaped mounts that make attractive arrangements for exhibition purposes.

Permanent displays

Special celebrations may be recorded with a permanent display. When displays of this kind

Using different shaped mounts adds interest to a display.

Examples of different shaped mounts

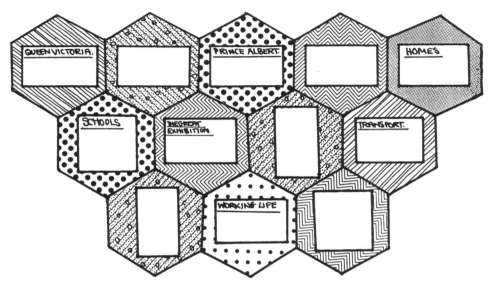

Mounts covered with different materials to form a 'patchhwork' effect.

A street scene created in clay

are planned, specific locations around the school will have been identified and set aside, and materials carefully selected as they will need to be durable and withstand regular cleaning. Relief work, using such materials as wood, clay, mosaic or fabric, is most suitable as it can be screwed, glued, or hung directly onto walls.

In one primary school in which I taught a fascinating street scene was created by the children using clay. It was glued to the walls, just above the skirting level, of the corridors leading to the main assembly hall. The completed display was a permanent reminder of the work of one particular year group and gave much pleasure and inspiration to other children in the school and the many visitors who remarked on it as they arrived at the school.

Displaying on exterior walls

I should also mention the considerable opportunities for developing permanent displays on the exterior walls of school premises. I dealt with this at some length in my previous publication, *Ways to Display*; but would like to emphasise again the great impact made by the painted murals and ceramic panels that brighten many drab school buildings around the country. Some schools do not even consider this possibility because they are worried about vandalism. But some of the most impressive and exciting work of this kind has been on the walls of inner city schools, with not a trace of vandalism to be seen — an indication, perhaps, of the kind of respect and care that children have for each other's work when high standards of display and presentation are considered an integral part of the school's philosophy.

Helpful Hints

The intention of this chapter is to suggest a number of additional time and labour saving ideas that will help teachers to achieve successful displays.

Big books and handmade books
Use flat sheet packaging to make the covers of 'Big Books' and the children's own handmade books. This can be obtained with little effort and no cost and yet is perfectly suitable for the task.

Drapes, backcloths and table coverings
Old plain, worn, or torn sheets and pillowcases can be dyed (using cold water dyes or Brusho color) and used to make attractive drapes, backcloths, and table coverings. If preferred, they can be block printed or decorated with batik or tie and dye designs before use. Many unsightly areas can be enhanced by the imaginative use of pieces of fabric.

Using jars, tubs and containers
Plants and flowers are to be greatly encouraged in classrooms and other parts of the school, but there is little more off-putting than to see them arranged in jamjars and plastic margarine tubs. There are various ways of improving their appearance.

1. Cardboard tubes or plastic drainpipe of a suitable diameter, cut into short lengths and covered with bright and attractive papers or self-adhesive plain or patterned vinyl sheeting (Fablon, Contact) can be slid over the jars to make them visually more attractive.

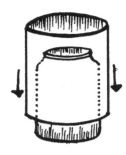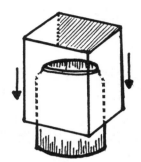

2. Similar disguise can be achieved by scoring and folding strips of thick coloured card, forming squares and rectangles that can be placed as 'sleeves' over jars and plastic containers. Improvements of this kind can make a considerable difference to the general appearance of a classroom.

3. Plastic containers such as ice cream tubs make excellent storage holders for small objects in the classroom but are not very attractive. They can easily be improved by cutting out shapes, letters, symbols, etc, from coloured self-adhesive film and then sticking them on the surface of the containers. If particular pictorial images are required they can be obtained by drawing with spirit-based (permanent) overhead projector pens/markers on transparent self-adhesive film. A set of similar containers, clearly identified, for storing such items as pencils, felt-tipped pens, scissors, crayons, etc, does much to help maintain good classroom management and standards of general tidiness.

Fixings
Many excellent displays are spoilt by using drawing pins to hold work onto the display boards. It is best to avoid them altogether if at all possible, as they are rather unattractive and their reflective heads can dominate a display and distract attention from the work being shown. If alternative fixings are not available and drawing pins have to be used, cover the head with coloured self-adhesive stickers so that the pins merge in with the colour of the work being displayed. This considerably improves the overall visual appearance of the display.

Staple guns
Whilst the use of staple guns (Trigger Tackers) greatly increases the speed at which two-dimensional work can be displayed, the situation is very different when the work needs to be removed. The force of the 'gun' causes the staples to be inserted flush with the surface of the board to which the work is being attached, leaving nothing protruding to grip hold of when trying to remove the staples. The most practical solution to the problem is to tape a small pad of cardboard to the base plate of the staple gun immediately behind where the staple emerges. This prevents the staple from being forced flush to the surface, leaving just sufficient protruding to grip. The visual appearance of the display is not adversely affected but much time is saved when dismantling.

Displaying on glass
Many teachers ask me about overcoming the frustrating problem of displaying work

on glass without it falling off. There is no perfect answer to this problem as it depends on the conditions — bright sunlight or severe condensation will affect the holding power of most materials. In shady, dry conditions display putty (Blu-Tack) will be satisfactory for a reasonable length of time, but where conditions are more variable Cowgum is much more likely to give better results. A small dab on each corner will hold work that is not too heavy and it is easily removed from the window with little more than a firm rub or at the most a small amount of white spirit or lighter fuel. (Keep both of these items stored out of the reach of children.)

Ceiling hooks

In many more recently built schools the classroom ceilings are of a panel construction, resting in criss-cross metal bars. This makes fixing mobiles or other hanging work from the ceiling particularly easy because locating points can be left in position for regular use rather than having to re-establish them every time hanging displays are to be featured. By lightly lifting the panels, neat soft bent wire hooks can be inserted where the metal resting bars cross.

Magnetic strip

In schools that have a considerable amount of metal in their construction (window frames, pillars, etc) magnetic strip, which is available from most educational suppliers, is a very useful alternative fixing. It can be cut into small pieces and either attached to the back of work or simply placed over the top of work to be displayed on a metal backing. It can help to extend display possibilities by bringing into action spaces that would otherwise not have been used. It will, of course, only hold lightweight work.

Things to avoid

Try to avoid displaying work in poorly lit areas where children are likely to show little interest in it. Clip-on spotlights are inexpensive to buy and are useful as additional light sources in dark and dismal areas.

Try not to display work too near to sinks, where it is almost certain to be splashed and therefore spoilt. If this cannot be avoided, use waterproof drawing inks for labels, captions, headings, and colour work to prevent the risk of colours running.

Avoid overlapping work. Space is an important element of good display. If overlapping is necessary so that more work can be shown, then it is likely that far too much work is being included.

Avoid displaying work at peculiar angles — it makes viewing difficult and generally off-putting. Work that is mostly executed on square or rectangular paper is best suited to a vertical and horizontal display arrangement. Avoid using drawing pins. They dominate displays because of their reflective qualities and are consequently very distracting to the viewer.

Focussing attention

Work requiring a specific focus in a display can be dealt with in a variety of ways in order to draw the necessary attention to it.

1. Mount the work differently from the other work being displayed, for example use a different coloured mount or triple mount the work if all the other work is double-mounted.

2. Place different coloured borders around sections of the display to focus attention on specific areas of interest and at the same time draw attention to their differences.

3. Use a small cardboard viewfinder to frame a particular area of interest in a piece of work so that the detail can then be displayed alongside.

4. Using a different shaped mount, for example circular, helps to focus attention on a particular piece of work.

5. Block mount a central piece of work to raise it from the surface in relief, thereby directing special attention to it.

6. Highlight a centrepiece by focussing a spotlight on to it.

7. Young children in particular enjoy the novelty of 'lifting a flap' or 'opening a door' to discover a new piece of learning.

8. The introduction of the novel, unusual or unexpected is sometimes the most successful way of securing interest and attention. Entrance and assembly halls often provide the scope for large scale displays of an unusual nature.

Such items as pieces of sculpture borrowed from a college of art to stimulate art and language work; large scale museum loans such as an old bicycle or examples of bygone domestic appliances to initiate a history project; or dummy figures dressed in historical costume or uniforms often act as starting points for topic work. It is surprising what can be borrowed if the school makes its needs known.

As a staffroom resource it is helpful to compile a list of contact persons and what they are prepared to lend. If each member of staff adds to the list as new contacts are made the document soon becomes a useful and time-saving asset.

Colour

Colour is an important factor in most displays. The choice of colours, the way in which they either contrast or harmonise, and the proportions in which they are used greatly influence the extent to which interest in a display is generated and its ultimate success.

Certain combinations of colours create problems in a display. Yellow, mounted on a white background, is often difficult to see at a distance. This is particularly so if yellow lettering is mounted on white.

Some colours clash violently, which makes reading and display almost impossible. The use of fluorescent colours makes particular difficulties in this respect. Contrasting colours, or those which harmonise, are usually very successful.

Plain backgrounds are always preferable to patterned ones and subdued colours more suitable than brightly-coloured ones, although there are, exceptions to this general principle.

It is often more effective to restrict the number of colours used in a display rather than introduce too many. A single colour mount used for all the work throughout a display is visually more pleasing than having each piece of work mounted on a different colour. The single colour approach adds a uniformity to the display that helps to hold interest.

Scale

Whilst most displays are viewed from a distance and therefore need to be of a suitable scale, some individual pieces of work need to be handled with sensitivity and mounted in such a way that they can be displayed in a place of their own, free from the distraction of other work too close to them. Provided that a piece of work is displayed appropriately there is scope for the small as well as the very big.

Assembly halls and other similar places require large scale work that may spread across the entire width or length of the room. Often this may be a composite picture, based on a selected theme, to which each class in the school may contribute. One which I viewed recently and greatly enjoyed was of a football match complete with life-size players, spectators, press photographers and policemen.

Another local primary school known to me organised a competition for its pupils to design a mural to 'take the school into the year 2000.' The creator of the winning design, aged 11 years, has recently completed painting the mural, assisted by some of his peers and a group of secondary-aged pupils. Overall it measures some three by four metres.

Mobile classrooms

Mobile classrooms present particular problems for display. Low ceilings, little wall space, windows on more than one side, and often cramped conditions, all mitigate against an environment that is visually attractive and that enriches children's learning. Whilst the following suggestions cannot claim to be ideal solutions, they are an attempt to provide practical help and ideas to improve a difficult situation. Wall space can only be created by 'blanking out' some of the windows (if the loss of light can be spared) and replacing them with floor-to-ceiling sheets of pinboard (Sundela), covered with paper-backed hessian.

Alternatively, the walls can be papered directly with hessian so that work can be attached without permanent trace of pinholes being left behind. This is a more time-consuming and expensive solution that might be adopted as a Parent Teacher Association project, but in the long term provides a much more inviting learning environment.

Pinboard, mounted at a 45° angle around the top of the walls, is another solution to providing increased display space for two-dimensional work. Although this is not an ideal height at which to display work, the fact that it 'slopes back' into the room helps to engage interest and make it visually acceptable.

In most mobile classrooms a boxed-in joist runs centrally along the full length of the room. Each side of this can be used as a display space, or alternatively mobiles or banners can be hung from it.

Work displayed on strings stretched across the width of a room can sometimes look unattractive and forgotten. However, in a situation fraught with difficulties, the value of hanging space cannot be underestimated. The best way to achieve a satisfactory result is to attach a screw eye into the wall on opposite sides of the room with another positioned in the underside of the central ceiling joist. String held and stretched between these three points remains taut and will readily support work without too much unsightly sagging. Work can be hung from the strings using Turikan hook staples (see list of tools), which can be lightly bent over to prevent the work from slipping. Paper clips are perfectly adequate and fairly unobtrusive, especially coloured ones — or even coloured plastic clothes pegs, despite being rather large, are suitable in certain situations. Arrange work so that it does not obstruct vision to other parts of the room.

Useful Information

TOOLS

Staple gun (Trigger Tacker)
Available from most educational suppliers: E.J. Arnold & Son Ltd, Butterfly Street, Leeds 10; Hestair Hope Ltd, 51 Philips Drive, Royton, Oldham; Philip & Tacey Ltd, North Way, Andover, Hants SP10 5BA.

Eyelet hole punch
Dryad Ltd, Northgates, Leicester; Nottingham Handicraft Ltd, 17 Ludlow Hill Road, West Bridgeford, Nottingham NG2 6HD.

Turikan hook stapler
Panda Binding Systems, 426 Wakefield Road, Denby Dale, Huddersfield HD8 8QD.

Ram or push pin tool
Available from most educational suppliers or locally from DIY stores.

Electric glue gun
E.J. Arnold & Son Ltd (address above)

Polystyrene cutter
B.S.T.E. Ltd, Carlton, Bedfordshire MK43 7LF; and locally from most DIY stores.

Rotary trimmers, craft scissors, craft knives, safety rulers, bambi staplers, staple removers, long arm staplers, etc, can be obtained from most educational suppliers or locally from office suppliers or DIY stores.

DISPLAY SYSTEMS/SCREENS
A full range of high and low cost systems can be obtained from: Marler Haley (Barnet) Ltd, 76 High Stret, Barnet, Herts; Buckley Displays Ltd, 5 Clevemede House, Reading, Berks; S.D. Systems Ltd, 375 Bath Road, Slough, Berks SL1 5QD

BACKING MATERIALS

Bargain bundles of hessian and felt
Warringer Warehouses, Station Road, King's Langley, Herts.

Hessian, felt, fabrics suitable for drapes and backgrounds
Dryad or Nottingham Handicrafts, or locally from market stalls, home decorating stores, or fabric stores.

Rolls of corrugated card (natural or coloured)
Available from Galt Educational, James Galt & Co Ltd, Brookfield Road, Cheadle, Cheshire SK8 2PN; also from Nottingham Educational Supplies and E. J. Arnold & Son Ltd. (E. J. Arnold also supply shaped border strips of corrugated card.)

Vivelle
A feltlike finished paper in a range of attractive colours. Available from Philip & Tacey, Nottingham Educational Supplies, and other educational suppliers.

Adhesives and fixings
PVA adhesive, glue pens, glue sticks (Pritt), double-sided adhesive pads, matt vinyl tape, coloured vinyl tape, mapping pins, coloured-headed pins, double-sided vinyl tape, gummed paper strip, masking tape — available from most stationers, office suppliers and educational suppliers.
Tough vinyl joining tape in wide widths, strong impact adhesives (Evostik, Bostik, Superglue) — available from most DIY stores.
Cowgum, copydex and other specialist adhesives — available from educational suppliers and graphic art suppliers.
Wallpaper paste (Polycell, Solvite) — available from DIY and home decorating stores.

Hand and stand magnifiers
(For placing over small objects in displays.) COIL, Combined Optical Industries Ltd, 200 Bath Road, Slough, Berks; Osmiroid Educational, E.S. Perry Ltd. Osmiroid Works, Gosport, Hants; and from most educational suppliers.

Shallow trays, storage containers
Available in a range of sizes and colours. G.P.G. Containers, G.P.G. International Ltd, Luton Road, Dunstable, Beds.

Pens and lettering aids
Stencils, mapping pens, marker pens, felt-tipped pens, fibre-tipped pens, dry mount lettering, lettering pens and nibs. Available from most leading stationers and office suppliers. Also from the following: Rotring — Werke Riepe KG, D — 2000 Hamburg 54; A. W. Faber — Castell, D — 8504 Stein, Nurnberg, West Germany (lettering/drawing pens); Coated Specialities Ltd, Chester Hall Lane, Basildon, Essex SS14 3BG (coloured self adhesive film).

Most art and display supplies can be obtained from: Berol Ltd, Oldmedow Road, King's Lynn, Norfolk PE30 4JR.

Material to Copy

On the following pages you will find a selection of material designed to be photocopied. Most of the material will need to be cut out, mounted on card, and coloured. The material will help to provide a co-ordinated labelling style both within individual displays and throughout the whole school. The finished products can be used either flat on two-dimensional displays or in sawcut blocks for use in three-dimensional displays. (See chapter: Lettering for Displays). The material is grouped in themes for convenience and is, of course, only a representative sample to provide teachers with ideas that can be developed in other ways. The 'tab' at the bottom of the shaped label cards is for placing in sawcut blocks to make them free standing and can be removed if the labels are to be used flat on a display board. The illustrations have been left as simple line drawings to enable teachers to colour them as they wish. Spaces have been provided in which teachers can print their own wording.

WEATHER SYMBOLS

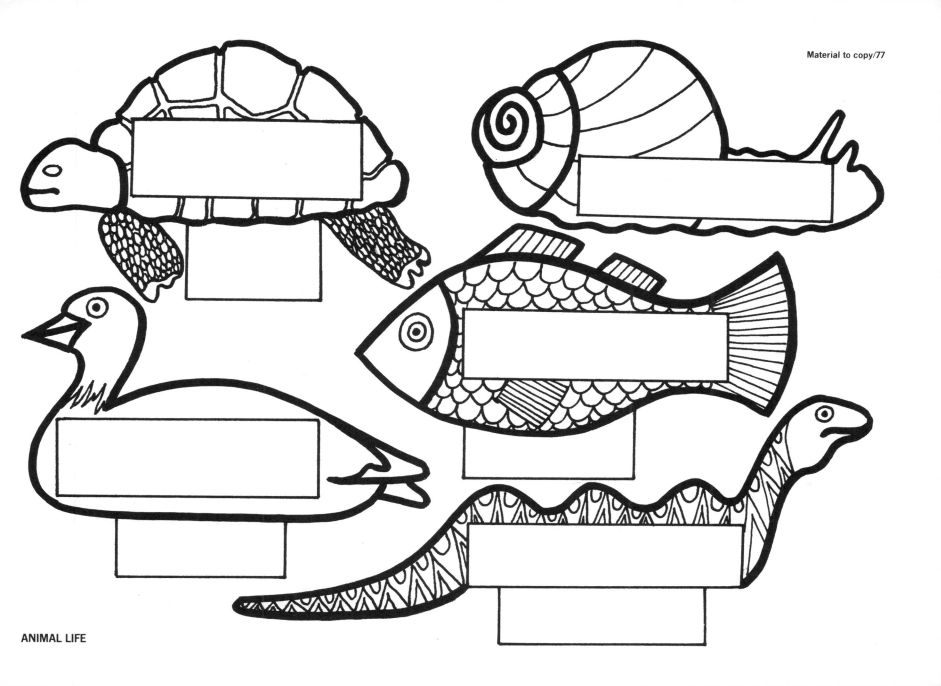

ANIMAL LIFE

TRANSPORT AND TRAVEL

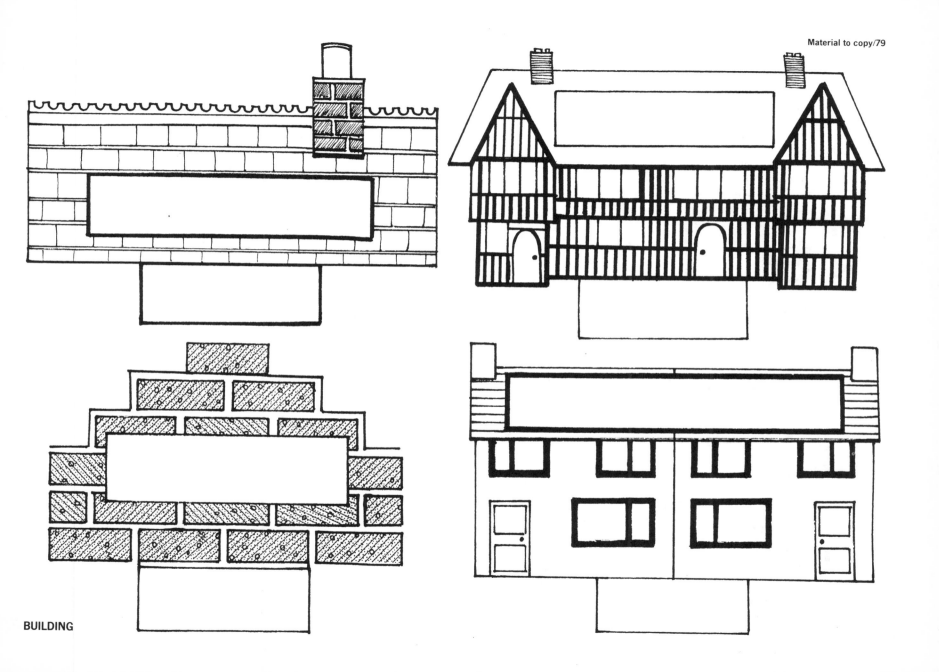

BUILDING

The following alphabet letters are provided as outlines for illuminated letters, to be decorated and used to enhance children's written work (e.g. making manuscripts or scrolls for historical writing, initial letters for story-writing, illustrated letter-writing, etc). They can be enlarged, if necessary, by copying them onto acetate and projecting them onto paper, using an overhead projector. Coloured pencils or drawing inks are recommended for decorating the letters.

ABCDE
FGHIJKLMNOP
QRSTUVWXYZ
1234567890